Handbook on human rights
and the rights of our earth

AUSSIE version

We sing songs for life:
Valuing people and the planet

Dr Julie Morsillo
Community Psychologist

SING ME A SONG TO SOAR
Finding Hope in Our Redemptive Stories

Copyright © 2025 Julie Morsillo. All rights reserved. Except for brief quotations in critical publications or reviews, no part of this book may be reproduced in any manner without prior written permission from the publisher. Write: Permissions, Wipf and Stock Publishers, 199 W. 8th Ave., Suite 3, Eugene, OR 97401.

Resource Publications
An Imprint of Wipf and Stock Publishers
199 W. 8th Ave., Suite 3
Eugene, OR 97401

www.wipfandstock.com

PAPERBACK ISBN: 979-8-3852-5666-2
HARDCOVER ISBN: 979-8-3852-5667-9
EBOOK ISBN: 979-8-3852-5668-6

Previous handbook on hope

Sing me a song to SOAR:
Finding hope in our redemptive stories
by Dr Julie Morsillo, Community Psychologist, 2024
Published with Wipf & Stock, December 2024.

My first reflective practical handbook for counsellors, or as a self-help book, was about helping ourselves and others to feel valued in life.

Life can be very challenging at times, with dark nights of the soul. We often need support to make our way through the tough times and find the light of the morning.

This reflective handbook offers some helpful tools to support others through their dark times, to find inspiration and hope in their redemptive stories for some healing. A hope that helps us find a story song to SOAR in life:

Stories of **personal meaning** in life with

Other **respectful relationships** beside us

A **supportive community** encircling us &

Restorative time in **nature**

This previous handbook provided some insights into uplifting hopeful narrative theories on finding personal meaning and ways to connect with others and with nature. It also included links to videos and further readings to learn more. Plus, some poetry and many practical worksheets with prompts, to help reflect on various aspects of life, as we seek to find more hopeful redemptive stories to soar in life.

> Weeping may last in the night,
> but there will be JOY in the morning (Psalm 30:5)

Dedication to children

To the millions of children in the world who are living in poverty, suffering fear in war-torn and unsafe places, with no haven, little food, healthcare, or education.

Through no fault of their own these children suffer. Children do not choose their country or the leaders of their world.

We need to reach out to them and offer a light of hope.

Richest men deny food to poorest children

The world's richest men take on the world's poorest children by Nichalas Kristof in New York Times
www.nytimes.com/2025/02/05/opinion/usaid-spending-trump-musk.html

USAID withdrawal affects Sudanese children – www.youtube.com/watch?v=GFSdpShtFEg

Gaza's starving babies – https://theconversation.com/images-of-gazas-starving-babies-have-gone-round-the-world-this-is-what-malnutrition-does-in-the-first-1-000-days-of-life-257462

Children starving in Gaza video – www.youtube.com/watch?v=dODVLt-x86Y

We sing songs for life:
Valuing people & the planet

Handbook on Rights Outline

This handbook is about advocating for human rights and the rights of the planet. A guide for community workers and others who are compassionate, wanting to meaningfully give to community, to improve the common good and improve our common home, the planet.

Life can be very challenging for those who constantly face injustice. Those who live in poverty, in places with no haven, healthcare or education; or those who face injustice due to a difference in status. Asylum seekers, children, disabled, Indigenous, neurodiverse, women, and racial, ethnic, sexual or gender minorities can each suffer at times. We need to show compassion and advocate for their human rights.

We also need to care for the environment in which we live, so we all have a healthy place to live and breathe. We can care for our Mother Earth, so she can care for us, giving life to us all.

We can sing songs together, working in harmony to support others in need, to value the lives of all peoples and the life of the planet:

S – **Spend meaningful time** with others who also want to live a valuable life by showing compassion and advocating for justice to empower those in need, and leave a legacy.

O – Reaching out to connect with the **other**, those who are also different or diverse. Welcoming the stranger, connecting with kindness (not just with family) to those in need: the hungry, sick, bereaved, imprisoned, refugee, migrant, neurodiverse, other abled, and those of other cultures and other religions.

N – Advocating for those in **need**, who are lacking in basic human rights: women, children and families in war-zones, those suffering injustice, abused or neglected, entrapped or enslaved, including Indigenous peoples. A common people with common rights.

G – **Greening** of the planet to restore nature, locally and globally, by taking action to: create gardens and parklands, restore bush-land country, have a light footprint, and much more. This planet gives us life, and needs care, as it is our common home.

This handbook provides some insights into practical ways to support those in need, offering kindness and compassion, whilst advocating for their common human rights, both in our local communities and to international communities in particular need.

Plus, considers ways to support our local environment and the global environment, so we have a healthy planet for our children and grandchildren. A common home for all.

> **Show kindness and mercy** to one another;
> do not oppress the widow, orphan, alien, or the poor. (Zechariah 7:9-10)

CONTENTS

Handbook on Rights inspiration 7

WE SING SONGS FOR LIFE 9
Background 10

PART 1: SPEND TIME CREATING A MEANINGFUL LIFE 13
Meaningful Community ENGAGEMENT 15
Meaningful Indigenous practices 18
Celebrating Cultural Diversity 21

PART 2: WELCOMING THE OTHER WITH KINDNESS 24
Community agency CONNECTIONS 25
The Kindness Revolution 32
Connecting with the neurodiverse & other-abled (othered) 33
Mentoring young people 34
Supporting women prisoners 38

PART 3: ADVOCATE FOR UNIVERSAL HUMAN RIGHTS 39
Human Rights ADVOCACY 40
Universal human rights 46
Human rights and social justice advocacy in Australia 48
Human rights for Indigenous Australians 49
Human rights for migrants 53
Displaced seeking sanctuary 54
Gendered human rights 57
Human rights for disabled (other-abled) 58
Human rights for sexuality 59
Human rights for slaves 60
Human right for basic income 61
Global human rights & peacebuilding 62
Local Community Empowerment Programs 64

PART 4: CHALLENGE OF GREENING THE PLANET 71
Greening the planet ACTIONS 72
Appreciating the awe in nature 75
Indigenous connection to Country 81
Environmental Psychology 82
Activists caring for nature 84
Community gardens & sustainable food agencies 86
Greening the planet 87

REFERENCES 95
Acknowledgements 100

Handbook on Rights inspiration

In early 2025, a couple of the richest men on the planet, decided that millions of poor children and their families, with little food, health-care or shelter, dependent on USAID, were to be immediately denied all aid.

I could picture millions of children dying, because of the greed of a few ultra-rich people in the world, who have as much wealth between them, as the poorest billion people in the world, They could easily share some of their wealth, and support programs for others in need (More on Ultra-rich p.12)

Human rights of the poorest children, for basic food, health care, shelter, and safety are being denied. There is something horribly wrong when we know how to help others yet refuse due to our own uncaring greed.

Julie in Chinese Friendship Gardens, Sydney, beginning this handbook. March 2025.

As a child, I heard of others who are suffering in Sunday School, with Christian teachings of Jesus, reaching out and showing compassion to the outcasts of society, the *unclean* and disposed. Living in Papua New Guinea as a young adult, experiencing a community minded culture sharing their food and goods, compared to our Western more individual culture.

As a young mother, I was challenged to consider human rights, caring for my own two children and taking in foster children, wards of the state, who had lived very different lives with abuse or neglect. At the same time, learning of rights, studying an under-graduate degree in psychology, with units in sociology and childhood across cultures at Victoria University.

Working at the Victorian Equal Opportunity Commission, it was confronting realising that people can often suffer due to their: minority race, ethnicity, gender, sexuality, religion, disability or age. I was further confronted while on an exposure tour of Philippines visiting community agencies, and staying in a slum with fisher-folk.

As I studied a Master of Social Science (International Development) at RMIT, I learnt how colonialism decimated the Indigenous peoples of the countries they invaded. My PhD research in Community Psychology at Victoria University, was with vulnerable youth, living in disadvantaged communities: a social group questioning sexuality; and recently arrived refugees from the Horn of Africa engaged in a bridging program. Also, teaching Community Development and Psychology at the same time, further opening my eyes to diverse experiences with rights abuses.

Later, I counselled asylum seekers at the Asylum Seeker Resource Centre, which led me to feel guilty that I had been born in a safe place. They did not choose to be born in war-torn countries, or into persecuted minority groups. Some were told good was evil, such as starting a school for girls in a country where education for women was banned.

Working at Australian Psychological Society with Indigenous psychologists, researching ways to support Indigenous youth in crisis, was challenging. Through travel to Czech and other parts of Europe, I learnt more of the holocaust and the courageous people rescuing whom they could. Also, through teaching counselling and Indigenous studies, and regularly visiting a young woman imprisoned for a decade.

So I want to continue reaching out to others who are suffering, and advocate for their human rights that are not being met. Seeing more human rights abuse recently, led to the writing this handbook.

Why this handbook?

Rights being abused

I am writing this handbook, as a counter to the calls for rejecting those who are different to us, withholding material aid to countries decimated by colonialism and corruption, and refusing basic human rights to: the hungry and the sick; to refugees from war-torn places and unsafe places; and those with diverse sexual preferences and gender identities.

Advocacy for humans needed

This handbook seeks to provide some practical ways to advocate and promote basic human rights for all: children to elderly, white to black, free to enslaved, any religion and any ethnicity. We need to supply the basic needs of all: free healthcare and education; a universal wage and affordable housing; a physical and emotionally safety environment; food security and clean water; meaningful work with time for creative and relaxing activities; with plenty of time to rest. So all can experience social justice.

Advocacy for the planet needed

The planet needs care to undo the damage that humans have inflicted. This handbook will provide some ideas for ways to care for the planet so we have a sustainable future for coming generations. Mother Earth gives us life, so we need to keep nature alive, by regenerating the land and caring for the waterways and much more.

TheAdvocateFor
HumanRights.org

Hope for a better world

This handbook seeks to offer ways to keep hope alive. We can easily sink into hopelessness, when we look closely at all the suffering in this world, humans treating other humans with contempt, and trying to destroy the planet on which we live, and gives us life. However, we can hold hope, by working with other people who also want to see a better world, being prepared to stand up for those who are treated unjustly, working hard with others who also want to see meaningful changes in the world to make it a better place. I acknowledge that there are many different perspectives one can take in relation to spirituality and religion offering compassionate ways to live and care for others. I have taken a Christian and Australian Indigenous stance, from my own background and experience as a practicing Christian and a community psychologist who has worked with Indigenous psychologists to try and bring hope to communities with little hope, to work for justice for all.

We can make a positive difference in this world, in various ways at different stages of our life. At some stages of our journey through life, we might have little to give when filled with our own struggles, apart from say small donations to charity, although that too is a start. Then at other stages of our life, we may find we have more time, or can prioritise life, to make more time, to give a more significant contribution to the lives of others in more need. This could mean becoming involved in policy making and politics, directly or indirectly, while at other times we might become involved with community agencies and community groups to make a difference with solidarity. This gives strength in numbers towards a better world, and gives us hope, with others around us who also care for people and the planet. My hope is that this handbook will offer some practical ideas to keep hope alive, and ways to work towards social justice for all.

We sing songs for life

Music is the soul of life

Songs have been sung for centuries to advocate for human rights and the rights of the planet. We sing together for the common good of the community and for the common home of our planet. Music can be very emotive, offering comfort, courage and hope for a better world. [Singing helps humanity – https://pursuit.unimelb.edu.au/articles/5-ways-singing-helps-humanity]

1. We sing meaningful, peaceful, protest songs when we see human rights violated, such as:
   * **Amazing grace** how sweet the sound (John Newton)
   * **Blackbird** – *inspired by civil rights movement* (Paul McCartney)
   * **Lift up your voice and sing** – *Black Anthem for civil rights movement* (Johnston & Johnston)
   * **My city of ruins** – Come on rise up (Bruce Springsteen)
   * **We shall overcome some day** (Traditional)
   * **You're the voice** – sung by John Farnham (Reid, Ryder, Qunta & Thompson)

2. We sing songs of welcoming the stranger with kindness for the abused and displaced, such as:
   * **All are welcome in this place** – Let us build a place where love can dwell (Martin Haugen)
   * **Bridge over troubled waters** I will lay we down (Paul Simon)
   * **Brother, sister, let me serve you** (Richard Gillard)
   * **Finding a home** – We are pilgrims, we are strangers (Ross Langmead)
   * **Lean on me** when you're not strong, I'll be your friend, I'll help you carry on (Bill Withers)
   * **Make me a channel of your peace** – Prayer of St Francis (Sebastian Temple)
   * **May my life be a prayer** (Julie Morsillo)
   * **That's what friends are for** (Carole Bayer Sager & Burt Bacharach)

3. We sing songs of life and love, calling for human rights to those not valued in life, such as:
   * **Beauty for brokenness,** hope for despair – God of the poor (Graham Kendricks)
   * **Grateful: A love song to the world** (Nimo Patel & Daniel Nahmod)
   * **Heal the world –** (Michael Jackson)
   * **I believe** in the people of all nations (Andrea Bocelli)
   * **Imagine** all the people, living life as one (John Lennon)
   * **Light a candle instead of cursing the darkness** (Suzette Hertz)
   * **One World, one song** – World Hunger Day UK 2013 (Sullivan Duntra)
   * **Took the children away** (Archie Roach)
   * **Peace for a world that is crying** (Julie Morsillo)
   * **We are the world, we are the children** – USA for Africa 1985 (Michael Jackson & Lional Richie)

4. We sing songs of awe and inspiration for the goodness of life and of nature.
   * **All things bright and beautiful** all creatures great and small (Cecil Frances Alexander)
   * **One world** – I'm going to take care of the world (Becky Drake)
   * **Take care of the world** (Karen Daniel)
   * **What a wonderful world** (Bob Thiele/George Douglas & George David Weiss)

If you are interested, there are more SONGS for LIFE with links to videos, at the end of this handbook

> Never doubt that a small group of thoughtful, committed citizens can change the world. Indeed, it's the only thing that ever has. Margaret Mead (1901-1978)

Background

In this life, each of us need an inspiring song to sing. A song that captures our imagination and tells the story of what we value in life in order to soar: a life of personal meaning, with respectful relationships beside us, and a supportive community encircling us, with time to restore our souls in nature. We cannot reach soaring heights without these elements in our life. [See my first handbook – Sing me a song to SOAR: Finding hope in our redemptive stories]

Humans throughout the world want to be treated as valuable, with their basic human rights met. A place where each is treated with respect, having a voice, that is not silenced. A place where we don't feel trapped and disrespected. A place that can provide us a haven, a shelter from the storms of life, where we feel safe and supported. A place with adequate food and healthcare, education and employment, where we have some personal agency and treat each other with compassion and respect. We need to sing songs for life, love and courage to shape a better world, for the most vulnerable children of this world and their families. Life for the planet, our Mother Earth who gives us life, so we need to look after her.

In this new era of 2025, millions of lives are being drastically changed or annihilated. Basic human rights are being removed world-wide, at the whim of a handful of billionaires, to poorer and war-torn countries where sadly life is often regarded as cheap, but reaching into the developed world, instigated by some of the richest people in the richest countries of this world, those with a colonialist mentality. [Oxfam report www.oxfam.org/en/takers-not-makers-unjust-poverty-and-unearned-wealth-colonialism]

In days gone past, colonialism adversely affected so many (with ongoing effects still felt today), as the power-hungry took over Indigenous peoples lands world-wide. Plundering those lands for precious minerals and space to grow industry and wealth for the invaders who were already wealthy. Now this is happening more overtly again.

Colonialism and capitalism, that accompanies this power-hungry concept, has also gone yet another step forward, where the super-rich crave more wealth and more power, at the detriment of everyone else. Last year, the wealth of the 10 richest people globally, increased by AUD$150 million per day, while the billion or more poor peoples' become increasingly poorer with less and less support. [Oxfam report, 2025 www.oxfam.org.au/2025/01/takers-not-makers-how-billionaires-profit-while-billions-struggle/amp/]

Ironically, a couple of the richest people in the world, who have multiple billions of dollars in their power, want to take away the small amount of health aid given to the poorest millions for food and sanitation to keep them alive. Millions of children will die without this health aid.

Every human being deserves basic human rights of free health-care and a universal basic income. [Universal Basic Income -www.theguardian.com/society/article/2024/jul/14/money-for-nothing-is-universal-basic-income-about-to-transform-society]

The richest country in the world, has withdrawn support of the World Health Organisation, and withdrawn funds from health-care research. Research that helps to track deadly viruses and helps develop appropriate vaccinations. Medical nurses and doctors giving aid to the poorest countries, tell us that without aid and health research, deadly diseases will be allowed to flourish world-wide, creating the risk of another deadly pandemic [USAID & Health funding withdrawn - World Economic Forum - www.weforum.org/stories/2025/03/usaid-cut-threatens-global-health-and-other-top-health-stories/].

Also, increasingly, anyone who is different in any way can find themselves, increasingly, demonised. Like the fascists of Nazi Germany in the past, they are targeting anyone who is different due to their ethnicity, sexuality or religion, to demonise them or intimate that they are less than human. In Nazi Germany, the demonising was often focused on Jews, Gypsies, (Romanies), gay (different sexuality), disabled and those of the minority or Indigenous ethnic group or religion. This demonising ended up with tens of thousands, millions even, being annihilated. This not on happened in Europe, but was often used in colonised countries, where the local Indigenous peoples were all but been annihilated. Now, many asylum seekers are being demonised for daring to ask for asylum away from war-torn lands. Everyone deserves to feel safe and supported, no matter their race or creed. [More in Human Rights p.46-56]

Those different to the norm, whether by race or by displaying various forms of sexuality and gender, including trans-gender, are being belittled or cancelled, for daring to be creative and different to the white male heterosexual stereotype. Women too, are becoming objectified and violated once again, with rampant male dominated social media. The violent porn, sex trafficking, and misogynistic political leaders and social media influencers, encourage young men to abuse women and children, in all they do and say. [More in Human Rights p.57]

Aboriginal and Torres Strait Islander adults make up 2% of the Australian population, yet they constitute 27% of the national prison population, due to systematic oppression and abuse applied over generations, causing intergenerational trauma [More in Human Rights p.49-52]

Many people of colour, in the wrong place at the wrong time, can be incarcerated, sometimes without any due process, shipped to another country to be tortured, never to be seen again. Some forms of torture, have been designed by white psychologists to brutally hurt prisoners, until they confess to whatever they are supposed to be done, just to stop the harm, or die in the process. [Psychologists design torture - www.theguardian.com/us-news/2020/jan/20/guantanamo-psychologists-cia-torture-program-testify]

Much of this was going on before 2025, but now at a hugely accelerated rate, adversely affecting millions and millions more peoples world-wide. Anyone who is not rich, white, male, heterosexual and very conservative could suffer. Then more suffering, due to a probable impending recession, more international conflicts and wars and possible conscription, and why? To appease the greed of a few power hungry people. [See more on Ultra-rich over the page]

Suppression of the press, which was occupied in some countries for decades, is now being spread into the so-called free-world, by USA, one of the richest countries in the world. A supposed pillar of the free world. We need to sing songs of freedom. Freedom of the press. Freedom from being abused when your only fault is being the wrong, gender, colour, ethnicity or religion. [See more in Human Rights].

There is also the destruction of the planet, that will happen faster, now that most research, funding and world-wide climate change targets have been abandoned by USA. This withdrawal of care for the planet by a very rich country, could be followed by other countries. [See more in Greening].

So now is the time to step up, to take notice, to advocate for human rights for all peoples of the earth, and advocate to save the planet, so our children and grandchildren have a healthy place to live and breathe. Hence this handbook with ideas to promote and advocate for human rights and for the survival of the planet, called: WE SING SONGS for LIFE.

Ultra-rich, colonialism and poverty

Our world has become more and more polarised, with the rich becoming ultra-rich, while the poor become even poorer. Yet, research shows us that the happiest communities, the more peaceful communities, are those where the people are more equal, economically and socially *(see reference below)*. Here are some recent reports from Oxfam, a well-regarded international community agency, on social and economic inequity, with poverty issues, as discussed in previous section.

Takers not makers: How billionaires profit while billions struggle (Oxfam Report 2025)

- Extreme concentration of wealth: Globally, billionaire wealth grew by AUD $3 trillion in 2024, with the wealth of the 10 richest people increasing by AUD $150 million per day. Billionaire wealth is growing three times faster than the year before.
- Unfair systems of wealth creation: Most extreme wealth is unearned; 60% of billionaire wealth comes from inheritance, monopolies, and cronyism.
- Global inequality persists: The number of people living below the poverty line is the same as it was in 1990; 3.5 billion people, or 44% of humanity.
- The world's richest 1% now own 45% of all global wealth. The richest 1% in wealthy countries extracted AUD $46.1 million per hour from low-income countries in 2023, further entrenching global disparities.

Role of social and solidarity economy – www.sciencedirect.com/science/article/pii/S2452292924000304
Oxfam community agency report, Jan 2025
www.oxfam.org.au/2025/01/takers-not-makers-how-billionaires-profit-while-billions-struggle/amp/
The succession of the billionaire class by Prof Robert Reich – https://robertreich.substack.com/p/the-secession-of-the-billionaire

Takers Not Makers: The unjust poverty and unearned wealth of colonialism

Billionaire colonialism – The unearned nature of much of the extreme wealth of the ultra-rich is arguably a result of colonialism and its impacts. Today most billionaires still live in the rich countries of the Global North, despite these countries being home to just one-fifth of the global population.

Historical colonialism and the ruling class – Colonialism, and the ideas that underpinned it, allowed the exploitation of the working-class majority to be taken to an even greater level of extremity. Tens of millions of people across the world have suffered because the ideas of racism and white supremacy gave justification and moral license to unprecedented and systematic levels of brutality, exploitation, and, at times, extermination.

Oxfam report – www.oxfam.org/en/takers-not-makers-unjust-poverty-and-unearned-wealth-colonialism
MORE REFERENCES on billionaires and the ultra-rich at the end of this handbook.

Note on Dismantling DEMOCRACY & end of American EMPIRE

Dismantle democracy by systematically dismantling four core institutions that create a democracy: the press, the legal profession, university & business community.

Dismantling of democracy in USA by Prof Arjun Appadurai
www.theguardian.com/us-news/ng-interactive/2025/may/25/trump-american-democracy
Trump is dismantling democracy – US Senate video – www.youtube.com/watch?v=7aDbEmHo9Fo
Is this the beginning of the end of the American empire? – Sydney Morning Herald video –
www.youtube.com/watch?v=vWHkTLzeGPk

Part 1: Spend time creating a **meaningful life**

It's better to light one candle . . . than curse the darkness

S - Spending time with others who want a valuable meaningful life to leave a legacy. Spend more time talking with your family, friends, and colleagues about ways to live a valuable life. Counterculture to the greed of the super-rich. Instead, consider ways to live with integrity: share time and wealth; share stories of kindness; share food with others who care; plan ways to act in meaningful ways; and sing songs of compassion for others in our faith and cultural communities.
[There are more songs in Songs for life on Page 9 and at end of the handbook]

PRACTICE

Consider your personal meaningful values, such as, empathy for others in need:
sick, lame, imprisoned, infirm, migrant, elderly, children in care, or living in poverty.
[*The life you can save: How to do your part to end world poverty*, by Peter Singer, 2019]

Are you more competitive or co-operative - struggling to reach top of the heap (capitalism), or more communal sharing (socialism).

> **We shall overcome**
> We shall overcome, we shall overcome
> We shall overcome some day ...
> For deep in my heart, I do believe
> We shall overcome some day.
>
> *Song calling for human rights to overcome oppression

Accumulating wealth or tithing and sharing to support others in more need.

Consider – small is beautiful i.e. having a small footprint on the earth. [*Small is beautiful* book by EF Schumarcher (1973) – half a century on in Practical Action – https://practicalaction.org/who-we-are/small-is-beautiful/]

HERO

Young Australian on the Year 2022 – Dr Daniel Nour
Founder of Street Side Medics – with video
www.australianoftheyear.org.au/recipients/dr-daniel-nour#:~:text=Dr%20Daniel%20Nour%20%7C%20Australian%20of%20the%20Year

> We need leaders
> Not in love with **money**,
> but in love with **justice**.
> Not in love with **publicity**,
> but **in love with humanity.**
> Dr Martin Luther King Jr. (1929-1968)

Inspiring meaningful stories

Story of building a cathedral

People find inspiration to care for people and the planet with meaningful actions, in a variety of ways, such as: the values from their faith community and/or a particular Indigenous or ethic group; a political stance and/or feminist values and/or greening the earth values. We often work within our natural local community to think globally and act locally.

The story of three bricklayers shows the power of having a meaningful purpose in your life and your work.

After the great fire of 1666 that levelled London, the world's most famous architect, Christopher Wren, was commissioned to rebuild St Paul's Cathedral. One day in 1671, Christopher Wren observed three bricklayers on a scaffold, one crouched, one half-standing and one standing tall, working very hard and fast.

To the first bricklayer, Christopher Wren asked the question, "What are you doing?" to which the bricklayer replied, "I'm a bricklayer. I'm working hard laying bricks to feed my family." The second bricklayer, responded, "I'm a builder. I'm building a wall." But the third brick layer, the most productive of the three and the future leader of the group, when asked the question, "What are you doing?" replied with a gleam in his eye, "I'm a cathedral builder. I'm building a great cathedral to The Almighty."

The story of the three bricklayers is also a metaphor on the power of purpose, where the "cathedral builder," demonstrates a personal expression of purpose that transforms his attitude and gives a higher meaning to his work. Another term for purpose we use in ministry circles is "calling." For the first bricklayer, building the wall was a job. For the second bricklayer it was an occupation. For the third bricklayer, it was a calling.

Sacred Structures by Jim Baker - The story of three bricklayers
https://sacredstructures.org/mission/the-story-of-three-bricklayers-a-parable-about-the-power-of-purpose/

Story of the Phoenix - from Greek Mythology

This story symbolises the possibility of renewal, for a meaningful life.

The legendary phoenix is a large, grand bird, much like an eagle or peacock. It is brilliantly coloured in reds, purples, and yellows, as it is associated with the rising sun and fire. Sometimes a nimbus will surround it, illuminating it in the sky. Its eyes are blue and shine like sapphires. It builds its own funeral pyre or nest, and ignites it with a single clap of its wings. After death a fledgling phoenix rises gloriously from the ashes, renewed and reborn, and flies away.

Ancient Origins - Symbolism of the Mythical Phoenix Bird: Renewal, Rebirth & Destruction
www.ancient-origins.net/myths-legends/ancient-symbolism-magical-phoenix-002020

Meaningful Community ENGAGEMENT

Consider what kind of community or culture you might be hoping to contribute to? For example: By joining fee-free TAFE art certificate class, you might be hoping to participate to a culture where art and creativity is valued, where people enjoy lifelong learning, where free education is given by governments and appreciated by society, where one can have fun and connect with people from different walks of life, where people can do things for their own interests and personal fulfilment (not just paid work) i.e. meaningful creative activities.

Consider joining a meaningful local community group that promotes engagement with community and sharing. Check out:

- Faith Communities Council of Victoria – www.faithvictoria.org.au
- Australian Neighbourhood Houses – www.anhca.org
- Free TAFE courses in Victoria – www.vic.gov.au/free-tafe
- Community choirs – Community Music Vic –https://cmvic.org.au/groups
- Community Gardens Australia – https://communitygarden.org.au
- Community Health Centres, Victoria - www.health.vic.gov.au/community-health/community-health-directory
- Common Grace – on Jesus & Justice – www.commongrace.org.au
- Action Network – eg. Love makes a way – Christians advocating for asylum seekers – https://actionnetwork.org/groups/love-makes-a-way-australia

Think about your privilege

Rate your privilege

Compare yourself to homeless child living on a rubbish dump. What did you do to deserve a safe warm home with plenty of food and entertainment (TV, computer & phone) ?

What did the homeless child do wrong?

Does a child choose their family, country or leaders?

Privilege refers to a set of unearned benefits, advantages or immunities that an individual or group receives based on aspects of their identity, such as race, gender, class or sexual orientation. Often contributes to social inequality, with advantages to some while disadvantaging others, such as white privilege. Also, socio-economic privilege may allow the wealthy and better-educated more opportunities for advancement.

Helpful Professor, Chris Drew PhD – https://helpfulprofessor.com/privilege-examples/

On Privilege (book), by Julian Burnside AO QC – www.hachette.com.au/julian-burnside/on-privilege

Short story on privilege animation – On a plate – The Pencilsword – www.rnz.co.nz/news/the-wireless/373065/the-pencilsword-on-a-plate

Meaningful Creative Community ENGAGEMENT

A. Join a local group for community engagement and creativity:

- Creative group - art, choir, band, wood or metal workshop, book club, craft market
- Religious group ministry– eg. church, mosque, synagogue
- Sporting club or gym club or swimming club
- Extended family or friends picnics or games or bushwalking

Community and belonging - https://kathy-edersheim.medium.com/about-community-and-belongingness-512601fcf7fc

B. Learn a new skill locally:

- A neighbourhood house program – eg. computer skills, crafts, new language
- Art classes – eg. mosaic; pottery; watercolour, oil or acrylic painting
- Music classes – eg. singing lessons, choir, musical instrument, band.

C. Learn about a community agency promoting meaning for those who are struggling

- Food security – local foodbank, food hub, farmers market, food swap.
- Shelter – addressing homelessness – crisis housing, women's crisis centre.
- Health – community health centre, family planning, physical & mental health therapies.
- Education – tutoring service, adult education, open university.
- Loneliness – calling or visiting lonely, visiting aged care facility

Celebrating Neighbourhood Houses video – www.youtube.com/watch?v=4_CYWBRw7ss

Planner for your meaningful actions

Meaningful Community eg. Faith community, neighbourhood house, community garden, community choir	Community Engagement eg. Creative group, religious ministry, sporting group, active group	New Meaningful Skill eg. Art or craft classes, music classes or band, computer skills, new language	Community Agency eg. Food hub or farmers market, crisis housing, health therapy, educational service, visiting lonely

Inspiring meaningful hymn

This hymn, Beauty for Brokenness (God of the Poor), calls us to be compassionate to the poor. It was commissioned by the charity Tear Fund (whose outreach focuses on those in poverty) for their 25th anniversary. A very meaningful hymn to consider others who are struggling in life, and who lack basic human rights.

Beauty for brokenness (God of the Poor)

Beauty for brokenness, hope for despair, Lord, in the suffering, this is our prayer
Bread for the children justice, joy, peace, sunrise to sunset, your kingdom increase!

Shelter for fragile lives, cures for their ills, work for the craftsman, trade for their skills
Land for the dispossessed, rights for the weak, voices to plead the cause, of those who can't speak.

God of the poor, friend of the weak, give us compassion we pray,
Melt our cold hearts, let tears fall like rain, Come, change our love, from a spark to a flame.

Refuge from cruel wars, havens from fear, cities for sanctuary, freedoms to share
Peace to the killing-fields, scorched earth to green, Christ for the bitterness, His cross for the pain.

Rest for the ravaged earth, oceans and streams, plundered and poisoned,
Our future, our dreams, Lord, end our madness, carelessness, greed,
Make us content with, the things that we need.

Lighten our darkness, breathe on this flame, until your justice, burns brightly again
Until the nations, learn of your ways, seek your salvation, and bring you their praise

Graham Kendrick. Copyright © 1993 – Make Way Music – www.grahamkendrick.co.uk
Commissioned for Tear Fund (to end poverty) 25th anniversary. Scriptures: Psalms 107:1-43
Song played with lyrics – www.youtube.com/watch?v=pPvioAt5fq4

More Songs for Life on Page 9 and at the end of this Handbook

---

Only the development of **compassion and understanding**
for others, can give us the tranquillity and happiness we all seek.
(Dalai Lama)

Meaningful Indigenous practices

Dadirri - Deep Listening that is meaningful

by Miriam Rose Ungunmerr-Baumann AO, 2021 Senior Australian of the year

The Indigenous People of Australia have a depth of spirituality that can enrich our Non-Indigenous spirits in so many ways. One of these spiritual gifts is Dadirri. Elder, Miriam Rose, invites all Australians to embrace tradition of *Dadirri* or deep listening.

Dr Miriam Rose AO, an Aboriginal elder, artist and educator, shares the concept of quiet meditation, an Indigenous practice to find out who they really are, their purpose, and where they are going.

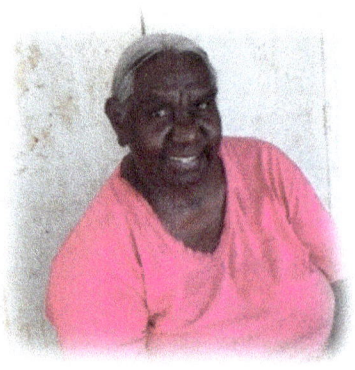

Dr Miriam Rose AO, Aboriginal elder, artist and educator.*

She calls it *Dadirri,* deep listening to the land. 'It's our make-up, it's our spirit,' she says. 'Sometimes our spirit is hurting or it is waning and we have to call on it to revive our drooping spirit. To do that, we say that *we call on the deep and the deep calls on us*, so we connect and feel that we belong still. And nature plays a part in your becoming a whole person.'

The tradition of Dadirri—deep listening to the land—is central to the spirituality of Miriam Rose Ungunmerr-Baumann and her people. These teachings are being adopted by some non-Indigenous Australian Christians, who see the practice as a step on a journey of reconciliation.

Rose, M. (2002). Dadirri: *Inner deep listening and quiet stillness.* Emmaus Productions.
*Photo used with permission from: Miriam Rose Foundation –
www.miriamrosefoundation.org.au/about-miriam-rose-foundation/

DADIRRI
Inner Deep Listening and Quiet Still Awareness

Acknowledgment of Country

We acknowledge that Aboriginal and Torres Strait Islander peoples are the traditional custodians and the first storytellers of the lands here in Australia. We honour Aboriginal and Torres Strait Islander peoples' continuous connection to Country, waters, skies and communities. We celebrate Aboriginal and Torres Strait Islander stories, traditions and living cultures; and we pay our respects to Elders past, present and emerging.

Acknowledgment of Country note

Acknowledgment of Country is an opportunity for anyone to show meaningful respect to the traditional owners of the land and to the continuing connection of Aboriginal and Torres Strait Islander peoples to their Country. This acknowledgment in some form is often stated at the beginning of meetings where there is a gathering of people for a meaningful purpose.

Acknowledgment of Country – Reconciliation Australia
www.reconciliation.org.au/reconciliation/acknowledgement-of-country-and-welcome-to-country/
Welcome to Country – by Aboriginal peoples to their particular country (within Australia)
Langton, M. (2019). Welcome to country: An introduction to our
first peoples for young Australians. Hardie Grant Publishing.
Murphy, J. W. (2016). Welcome to Country. Walker Books Australia. *(picture book)*

Songlines of meaning for Indigenous Australians

Australian Aboriginal peoples' ancestral stories and songs are unique ways to connect with their country and kin.

Songlines are the Aboriginal walking routes that crossed the country, linking important sites and locations. Before colonisation they were maintained by regular use, burning off and clearing.

The term *'Songline'* describes the features and directions of travel that were included in a song that had to be sung and memorised for the traveller to know the route to their destination. Certain Songlines were referred to as *'Dreaming Pathways'* because of the tracks forged by *Creator Spirits* during the *Dreaming*. These special Songlines have specific ancestral stories attached to them.

Songlines contain information about the land and how the traveller should respectfully make their trip. This includes the types of food that were safe to eat, places to be avoided and the boundaries of each *Mob's Country* (i.e. different Aboriginal nations with different language and traditions within Australia). that the traveller could pass through. Songlines also describe features and landmarks that the traveller should look out for, to know they are going in the right direction.

Songlines also act as a *'Cultural Passport'* when travelling through the country of another *Mob*. The verses that relate to a particular region, can be sung in the local language so that the people living there know that travellers are passing through in a respectful manner.

Aboriginal *songlines* helped form the map of Australia today. Aboriginal *star maps*, part of the songlines, are 'maps of the land', not maps of the sky. Star maps use celestial bodies as mnemonic devices (memory aids) to teach the route and physical and cultural waypoints of a journey. Stars may indicate where to veer north or south, for instance, or they may indicate the location of a freshwater spring.

Aboriginal Australian *star maps* are a part of songlines, a fascinating, complex method of navigation. "In Aboriginal mythology, a songline is a myth based around localised *'creator-beings'* during the *Dreaming*, the indigenous Australian embodiment of the creation of the Earth.

Each *songline* explains the route followed by the creator-being during the course of the myth. The path of each creator-being is marked in sung lyrics. One navigates across the land by repeating the words of the song or re-enacting the story through dance which, in the course of telling the story also describes the location of various landmarks on the landscape (e.g. rock formations, watering holes, rivers, trees).

Neale, M. & Kelly, L. (2023). *Songlines: Power and Promise.* First Knowledges Series. Thames & Hudson.
The Songlines Code: Margo Neale and Lynne Kelly – video - www.youtube.com/watch?v=gUcbbPS1z6E
Marlaloo Songlines video – Australia Institute of Aboriginal and Torres Strait Islander Studies
www.youtube.com/watch?v=rXbrOSDmUpg
Indigenous spirituality – Callaghan, P., & Gordon, P. (2022). *The dreaming path: Indigenous thinking to change your life.* Pantera Press
.Deverall, G.W. (2018). *Gondwana theology: A Trawloolway man reflects on Christian Faith.* Morning Star Press.
Deverell, G. W., & Pattel-Gray, A. (2023). *Contemplating country: More Gondwana theology.* Wipf & Stock.

Circle of Wellbeing with Indigenous Women
by Miriam Bevis and colleagues

The Circle of Wellbeing course was developed for Indigenous Kungas' women with trauma experiences, imprisoned in Central Australia, to help support them with hopeful stories and cultural stories and songs, for more hopeful lives.

The Circle of Wellbeing was a vital first step in the first days of a course with traumatised Indigenous women in Central Australia, to create a felt sense of safety for the women within the prison educational environment, while also providing deep cultural grounding. The women were told that when they entered the educational space of the prison each morning, they would be creating their own learning environment. To open the day, *Dadirri* by Miriam-Rose Ungunmerr-Baumann *(see previous pages)* was used as a reflective meditative practice. Creating feelings of safety for the group, and opening up the group to listening to others, and being heard, as part of this ceremonial cultural healing. Each morning, the women were invited to contribute with a word or sentence to reflect how they were feeling. In the beginning, the standard word was "good", which was what they believed they were expected to say. Some of the women were so shy they could not lift their heads, speaking in whispers.

They moved through the eight points of the Circle of Wellbeing:
1. Spirituality
2. Environment (land–spirit)
3. Relationships
4. Emotion.
5. Physical body
6. Sexuality, stress (culture in family wellbeing)
7. Life-purpose (identity)

While these were non-threatening conversations supported by scrapbooking, art and music, the women quietly reflected on deep inner hurt; eg, on issues around relationships, sexuality and loss of their children.

Meaningful safe boundaries for Indigenous women

The concepts of **anger, violence, boundaries, and safety** were based on meaningful conversations around the concerning issues of anger and violence, with the following specific learning modules:
1. Anger, violence, boundaries, safety (definitions)
2. Feelings—how we communicate
3. Anger triggers—the anger cycle, authentic anger, unauthentic anger
4. Parenting, being parented, parenting our children
5. Understanding the evolution of anger from childhood
6. Changing the game, parenting our children, parents as teachers
7. Hot violence (including rage), cold violence, assertiveness
8. Managing anger, breaking the cycle, alcohol and other drugs, gambling and jealousy
9. How violence affects children, families, communities
10. Cultural rules for safe expression of anger
11. Being assertive
12. Body scan, relaxation, mindfulness
13. Resilience behaviour, because a child living with distressed family behaviour can learn enabling adult behaviour, which deepens trauma.

Bevis, M., Atkinson, J., McCarthy, L., & Sweet, M. (2020). Kungas' trauma experiences and effects on behaviour in Central Australia (Research report, 03/2020). ANROWS. www.anrows.org.au/project/kungas-trauma-experiences-and-effects-on-behaviour-in-central-australia/

Celebrating Cultural Diversity

We can celebrate communities at their best, where there are shared values, such as: hospitality, honouring elders, family oriented, age-old traditions and songs for life. [For example: Gracias a la vida – Thank you for life – a popular Spanish song by Violeta Parra, a Chilian poet and activist – video – www.youtube.com/watch?v=jAlKfFLFnRI]

Indigenous cultures are close to country and kin, valuing sacredness of the land, honouring kinship ties, caring for environment, animals, plants, and medicinal plants to heal. Indigenous traditional rituals and understandings, learnt from respected elders, passed down through the generations.

Cultural festivals to celebrate spiritual and community values, music and dance and other movement and meditative practices (like kite flying and Chinese dragon, lanterns, flowers and lights at the graveside to remember those who have gone before us).

Sharing hospitality with others, offering food and drink with locally grown plants of diverse flavours and cooking styles.

Travelling offers a chance to make a new friend, different to us, while traversing and exploring.

Community gardening to provide fresh healthy foods to eat and sharing community connectedness.

Community choirs to celebrate folk music, often developed from mothers telling stories to children and singing lullabies, In the Brunswick Women's Choir we worked with several cultural groups to learn their traditional songs to sing and play with them in their language, at times accompanied by traditional musical instruments. [See: Seeking Harmony handbook by Brunswick Women's Choir – www.goodreading.com.au/books/book/21072/seeking-harmony-stories-from-the-brunswick-womens-choir/48]

Culture-based restaurants to appreciate enticing and spicy flavours and delicacies from around the world with different textures and smells and colours.

Celebrating special occasions of birthdays, and other rituals to mark or commemorate life transitions, like name days, baptisms, confirmation, special birthdays, weddings, or funerals.

Celebrating **sub-cultures** of various identities around sexuality and interests (like LGBTQi+, Gothic, game players, heavy rock and more).

Music festivals – ethnic-based world music, folk, traditional, classical, jazz, popular and more

Dance festivals – folk dancing, ballet, tap, modern, waltz, square dancing, line dancing and more

Art, design, photography and fashion exhibitions and shows - various ethnic groups, various styles from realistic to abstract.

Expressions of ethnic group-based **faiths and spirituality** – from Buddhist mediation and yoga, to Muslim daily prayer times facing Mecca, to Christian Sunday worship with music and prayers and readings - hopefully each at their best, showing compassion to others.

Victorian Multicultural Commission

Support and advocacy for culturally and linguistically diverse Victorians, engaging with multicultural and multifaith groups to understand the issues they face. Working together to identify and recommend potential solutions to government, policymakers and community organisations to make public services more inclusive and accessible.
www.multiculturalcommission.vic.gov.au

Grace to create meaning and dignity in life

In her book on grace, **Bright shining: How grace changes everything**, by Dr Julia Baird details how having grace can create a meaningful and dignified life.

Julia Baird suggests: "Grace is both mysterious and hard to define. It can be found when we create ways to find meaning and dignity in connection with each other, building on our shared humanity, being kinder, bigger, better with each other.

"Grace is . . . forgiving the unforgivable, favouring the undeserving, loving the unlovable. But we live in an era when grace is an increasingly rare currency. The silos in which we consume information dot the media landscape like skyscrapers, and our growing distrust of the media, politicians and public figures has choked our ability to cut each other slack, to allow each other to stumble, to forgive one another."

Baird. J. (2023). *Bright shining: How grace changes everything*. Fourth Estate Australia.

Feeding the soul

I wrote the following poem about feeding our souls to enable us to give grace to others.

We need to feed our own souls, support the lost souls of others
Feed our soul with good thoughts

Time away from business & worry.
Time in peaceful nature, meditation and reflection
Learning to have more empathy, following the example of Jesus
Compassion towards the sick and lonely.
Be fed by a mentor and trusted friends, to reflect debrief, and learn
Plan holidays and mini-holidays, time with friends and family
So no compassion fatigue or vicarious trauma.
Fill our minds with positive affirmations,
Say no to negative soul destroying thoughts from shame and guilt experiences
Keep a gratitude journal recalling small pleasures,
Have a worry time, that is contained, to have a plan,
Say no to self when worry at other times,
Bite your tongue when negative words come,
Build each other up, affirmation and appreciation
Work on a goal of being creative
Enjoy creative music and art, craft or garden, make something
Care for our body like a temple, only one body that can't be replaced
Eat healthy, keep hydrated, be active, rest well.

> Whatever is:
> true & noble,
> right & pure
> lovely & admirable
> excellent or praiseworthy
> Think about such things.
> (Philippians 4:8)

Amazing grace

SONG of GRACE - An iconic song on how grace creates meaning in life, was composed by a former slave-trade owner, John Newton. He changed his life around, towards a more caring and meaningful life, and wrote the song: Amazing Grace.

Amazing grace history – www.cbsnews.com/news/the-story-of-amazing-grace/

Note: **Grace road** - another song of grace, saying sorry to Indigenous peoples by Philip Hudson
For Sorry Day 2016 – www.youtube.com/watch?v=-Mo_OUsblMc

Personal meaningful memories - nostalgia

> **NOSTALGIA**
> Greek word meaning: return and pain

Meaningful memories from the past, including music attached to those memories, can be comforting or inspiring, even though often bitter-sweet. We can feel nostalgic thinking of past meaningful memories to inspire us towards a meaningful future.

Nostalgia is a sentimentality for the past, typically for a period or place with happy personal associations. But the memories might also be painful, since life often brings change accompanied by some kind of grief and loss or aging. However, remembering the good stories, the preferred stories, the stories of hope, can be helpful.

Hepper et al. (2012) found that laypersons view nostalgia as a bittersweet, but primarily positive, emotion arising from fond and personally meaningful memories that usually involve childhood or close relationships. Nostalgia often entails rose-tinted views of the memory, missing it, and a desire to return to the past; one typically feels sentimental and happy with a tinge of longing (Hepper et al., 2012).

Nostalgia has regulatory properties. Individuals spontaneously turn to personal nostalgia for comfort and strength in the face of psychological threats, and inducing it confers psychological benefits (Routledge et al., 2013)

For example, experimental and cross-sectional studies show that individuals recruit and experience nostalgia in times of loneliness, discontinuity, and existential doubt (Routledge et al., 2011)

Nostalgia then repairs and enhances social connectedness, self-regard, and meaning in life (Routledge et al., 2011)

> Hepper, E. G., Wildschut, T., Sedikides, C., Robertson, S., & Routledge, C. D. (2020). Time capsule: Nostalgia shields psychological wellbeing from limited time horizons. *Emotion. American Psychological Association.*
>
> Routledge C., Arndt, J., Wildschut, T., Sedikides, C., Hart, C., Juhl, J., Vingerhoets, A. J., & Scholtz, W. (2011). The past makes the present meaningful: Nostalgia as an existential resource. *Journal of Personality and Social Psychology*, 101, 638-652.

> Should old acquaintance be forgot

An old popular nostalgic song is *Auld Lang Syne – Should old acquaintance be forgot*
www.youtube.com/watch?v=zirXXRPi0V4

NOTE: Creating meaningful community project with vulnerable youth to create nostalgic memories in my PhD research – Morsillo, J & Fisher, A. (2007). Appreciative inquiry with youth to create meaningful community projects. The Australian Community Psychologist, 19, pp.47;61.

Part 2: Welcoming the other with kindness

O – Other – Reaching out to the other, those who are different, diverse, the stranger (not just family). Welcoming the other with kindness and meaningful connection: the hungry, sick, bereaved, imprisoned, refugees, migrants, neurodiverse, transgender, other abled, elderly, and those of different cultures and religions.

Consider ways to spend more time talking to, caring for or writing about those different to ourselves, and those who often struggle with injustice in everyday life.

The highest form of wisdom is kindness

PRACTICE

Hero – Dame Jacinda Ardern, former Prime Minister of New Zealand, hugging Muslim women after terrorist attack (& refusing to name the attacker or show videos of the attack) – *April 2019.*

Iconic image on Melbourne silo of NZ leader Jacinda Ahern
www.sbs.com.au/news/article/iconic-image-of-nz-leader-jacinda-ardern-to-feature-on-melbourne-silo/88e0efg8r

A different kind of power: A memoir by Dame Jacinda Ardern (2025) Penguin. Interview with Oprah – www.youtube.com/watch?v=8j3xM-GdS3E

> It takes courage and strength to be empathetic, and
> I'm very proudly an empathetic and compassionate leader
> Dame Jacinda Ardern (2025)

Community agency CONNECTIONS

Consider **creating connections** through involvement with a caring community agency, such as:

- Good Shepherd – Youth Homelessness https://goodshep.org.au/services/youth-homelessness-service-vic/
- Local food hub – Open Food Network – Merri Food Hub https://openfoodnetwork.org.au/merri-food-hub/shop
- McKillop Family Services – www.mackillop.org.au
- Mission Australia – Christian charity for safe homes – www.missionaustralia.com.au/about-us
- NDIS peer support (National Disability Insurance Service) – www.ndis.gov.au
- Prison Network – supporting women in prison & post-prison – www.prisonnetwork.org.au
- Sacred Heart Mission – Australian charity to end homelessness – www.sacredheartmission.org
- Smith Family – Australian children's charity supporting education – www.thesmithfamily.com.au

Consider **celebrating diversity** at local festivals and talkfests.

- Centre of Culture, Ethnicity & Health – www.ceh.org.au/harmony-day-march-on/

Consider attending an event celebrating diversity, such as:

- University of Melbourne – Celebrate Australia's diversity over the summer – https://pursuit.unimelb.edu.au/articles/tis-the-season-to-celebrate-australia-s-diversity

*Planner for **acts of kindness and connection***

Community agency kindness eg. ASRC, ARC, Food Hub, Services for families, homeliness, education, NDIS, prison network	Local community development eg. Playgroups, tutoring, book club, community choir, community garden, peer support	Local community service eg. Anglicare & other community agencies, charities for food, education & shelter	Local neighbourhood support eg. Offering support to neighbours, share clothes, street party

Community group CONNECTIONS

A. **Participate** in a local community development project

- Community garden
- Community choir
- Book club
- Neighbourhood House
- Playgroup for toddlers
- Read stories to children in library
- Pre-schoolers music group
- Peer support for neurodiverse
- Tutor a school student
- Learn a new language

B. **Volunteer** in a local Community service agency, such as:

- Op Shop (Opportunity shop)
- Visiting lonely elderly
- Offering Respite Care
- Offering Foster Care

C. Find ways to provide small acts of kindness and connection – like Boy Scouts & Girl Guides are taught to do – make cookies and share, mow lawns, fix something for a neighbour. [Helping others is good for well-being - Strong relationships, strong health – www.betterhealth.vic.gov.au/health/healthyliving/Strong-relationships-strong-health]

D. **Vocation** in community service, such as:

- Anglicare Australia – www.anglicare.asn.au
- Country Women's Assoc - https://cwaofvic.org.au
- Uniting Housing – www.unitinghousing.org.au
- BaptCare – www.baptcare.org.au
- Catholic Healthcare – www.catholichealthcare.com.au
- Uniting Care – https://unitingcare.org.au
- Settlement Council of Australia – https://scoa.org.au/who-we-are/
  [see more in ACTION previous page]

E. **Be involved** in local neighbourhood support or celebrations together, such as:

- Visiting lonely or unwell neighbours
- Helping in practical ways - take food and flowers when sick, mow lawns, take out bins,
- Offering support - babysit kids, swap clothes, swap scraps for chook eggs, exchange clothes,
- Community garden
- Street party [**Street party** for connecting neighbours - ABC News, 2022 – www.abc.net.au/news/2022-12-23/neighbourhoods-encouraged-to-organise-street-parties/101804694]

Consider celebrating the resistance efforts of people who are Othered by our society. People who are treated differently in our society, are always responding to and resisting the hardships they experience. We can walk alongside them, such as in the cultural diversity events. e.g. by donating, by promoting their programs and groups, by sharing their books and watching their movies, by sharing their strengths in conversations.

Acts of connection with kindness in community

Welcoming the Stranger

Personal Story of kindness from San Francisco

A most treasured memory from one of my visits to USA, comes from a Martin Luther King Sunday in 2003. My husband and I were in the USA, as he was to attend a conference, and I was researching my PhD. On Martin Luther King Sunday we went to the Second Baptist Church, San Francisco, a primarily African-American congregation, which were having a special annual service with the local Jewish Synagogue congregation.

The church and the synagogue congregations worked together all year long to provide tutoring to poor students to help them get into university. The service was amazing, with the Rabbi preaching and saying how much he enjoyed the Baptist congregation because they showed their appreciation more, with their loud *Amen brother* and *Hallelujah* through the sermon. Of course, the choir and the organ were good too. I remember singing the hymn, the black anthem: Lift every voice and song [See more in Songs for Life at the end of handbook].

Then at the end of the service, we were invited to stay for lunch. There were only limited seats around round tables, while most had to stand or sit around the edge of the hall. However, we noticed they invited the old ladies, the widows, to be seated first. Then they invited us, my husband and I to sit down too at the tables (20 years ago were we not too old!).

We asked them why? We were told, because you are the stranger, the other whom Jesus told us to care for and welcome the widows, the sick and the stranger, those who are different to us.

We were truly humbled to be given a seat at their table.

Universal compassion

This quote about Jesus, from a Jewish man, who had been immersed in different religions, impressed me.

The late Leonard Cohen – singer and composer, prophet and philosopher, poet and author, Jewish and Buddhist monk – showed an interest in Jesus as a universal compassionate figure, saying:

'I'm very fond of Jesus Christ. He may be the most beautiful guy who walked the face of this earth. Any guy who says 'Blessed are the poor. Blessed are the meek' has got to be a figure of unparalleled generosity and insight and madness ... A man who declared himself to stand among the thieves, the prostitutes and the homeless. His position cannot be comprehended. It is an inhuman generosity. A generosity that would overthrow the world if it was embraced because nothing would weather that compassion. I'm not trying to alter the Jewish view of Jesus Christ. But to me, in spite of what I know about the history of legal Christianity, the figure of the man has touched me'.

Jim Devlin, 1999. *Leonard Cohen: In his own words.* Omnibus Press. p.96.

Courage and Kindness in troubled times

> **Kindness in another's trouble,
> Courage in your own**
> Adam Lindsay Gordon quoted in
> Webb, C. (2006). To some, Gordon legend stands like stone. *The Age newspaper*. 24 June, 2006. www.theage.com.au/national/to-some-gordon-legend-stands-like-stone-20060624-ge2l1q.html

> "One isn't necessarily born with courage,
> but one is born with potential.
> Without courage we cannot practice
> any other virtue with consistency.
> We can't be kind, true, merciful, generous, or honest."
> Maya Angelou quoted in James, M. (2017). *Making of a phenomenal woman*. Friesen Press.

Kindness may seem a simplistic virtue but can be powerfully applied. Fanciful assumptions equating kindness with generosity can be challenged in a familiar story, *The Prodigal Son*, where the story is presented from the perspective of virtues as opposed to the subjugating morality of patriarchy.

Generosity, with its susceptibility to self-interest, can be considered merely a means to kindness. However, that kindness can be fuelled by compassion. That compassion, exemplified in successful foster carers, requires entering another's suffering, thereby giving of oneself. Herein lies the power of kindness, able to "change the quality of the suffering".

Edwards, T., & Chiera, C. (2019). *The freedom of virtue: Navigating excellence in the art of living amongst a world of instant gratification*. Australian Academic Press Group.

Collective charity and kindness

A virtuous community could be imagined as one of kindness and courage. Taking courage in both hands to do what needs to be done to build a strong community, with kindness as the key.

We need to foster the concepts of collective pain in times of hardship, and collective celebration in times when we have weathered hardship, with a sense of collective charity and kindness.

Costello, T. (2020). We need to be physically distant but we need to share our collective pain. The Guardian, 30 March, 2020. www.theguardian.com/world/2020/mar/30/we-need-to-be-physically-distant- but-we-need-to-share-our-collectivepain?CMP=Share_iOSApp_Other

Connecting in the darkest of times - Auschwitz

Kitty's story of courage and kindness in Auschwitz

This historical narrative, out of the depths of despair, exemplifies the connections of courage and kindness of human nature in the face the most terrible of trials and tribulations.

The women of the Auschwitz concentration camp in Poland, during the occupation of Nazi Germany, suffered unimaginable cruelty. Yet, these women responded to their predicament, by forming little families for mutual support. These women bonded with each other, like can be seen in the animal kingdom, to support each other.

Perhaps it was altruism, but also a matter of survival. To be alone in Auschwitz was to place your life at great risk. Without someone to help you out from time to time, it was virtually impossible to survive for long in that death-camp.

Little families formed within a block, with three or four becoming friends, who would stick together and organise things together. One might acquire some bread, another might find a handkerchief or a pencil and some scraps of paper, another a mug of water, to share with the group.

Members of a group helped each other and defied the rest. Outside the family there had to be bribery, but within there was love and mutual help and support.

*Grunwald-Spier, A. (2019). *Women's experiences in the Holocaust: In their own words.* Amberley Publishing

Video of another kindness at Auchwitz
www.oundleschool.org.uk/past-events/kindness-a-legacy-of-the-holocaust/

Note on **connecting communities** in darkest times

Narrative therapists and community workers at Dulwich Centre, Adelaide, have a practice of connecting communities who have suffered greatly, including genocide survivors, in order to strengthen resilience and resistance, to bring some hope.

Strengthening resistance: The use of narrative practices in working with genocide survivors
https://dulwichcentre.com.au/wp-content/uploads/2018/06/Strengthening-resistance-extract.pdf

Working with memory in the shadow of genocide: The narrative practices of Ibuka trauma counsellors
by David Denborough – https://dulwichcentre.com.au/product/working-with-memory-in-the-shadow-of-genocide-the-narrative-practices-of-ibuka-trauma-counsellors-david-denborough/

Documenting people's skills and knowledge videos
https://dulwichcentre.com.au/courses/aboriginal-narrative-practice-course/lessons/05-documentation/

> My wish for you is that you continue.
> Continue to be who and how you are,
> to astonish a mean world with your **acts of kindness**.
> Continue to allow **humor** to lighten
> the burden of your tender heart.
> Maya Angelou (1928-2014)

Connections with asylum seekers
Power of hope for a community of love and compassion
by Kon Karapanagiotidis AOM, founder & CEO of the Asylum Seeker Resource Centre.

The power of Hope (2018), written by Kon Karapanagiotidis, the founder of the Asylum Seeker Resource Centre, argues that by putting community, love and compassion at the centre of our lives, we have the power to change our world.

The Asylum Seeker Resource Centre (ASRC) in Melbourne, is a virtuous community, coming together and connecting in times of need.

I worked at the Asylum Seeker Resource Centre as the Counselling Co-ordinator, a number of years ago, and it was the most inspiring experience, with hundreds of volunteers and low-paid co-ordinators, supporting asylum seekers with kindness and with many practical supports, including: free health care, counselling, case work management, legal advice, foodbank, lunch every week day prepared and eaten together, empowerment support, English classes, fun activities for families, and much more.

Each day it felt like working in an amazing intentional community. The founder, Kon Karapanagiotidis (2018), gathered us together each morning and gave us an inspiring talk and update, as the motivating leader.

A wonderful example of creating a virtuous community of kindness and compassion, to give practical and meaningful support to asylum seekers in need, by providing basic human rights to help survive life after trauma and to find hope once again.

The ASRC founder, Kon, has written a book on his personal experiences and that of the ASRC, called *Power of Hope: or how community love and compassion can change the world* (Karapanagiotidis, 2018)

"I hope you take from this book the message that we all matter. That there is a place for all of us. That once we know our own voice, live the values close to our hearts and follow our dreams, we can be unstoppable. Hope is only exhausted if we forsake ourselves, otherwise no one can take hope away from us. It is both our sanctuary and our destiny to live a life with love, belonging, connection and community."

Karapanagiotidis, K. (2018). The power of hope. Riverhead Books. Harpers Collins Publishers.

Kon Karapanagiotidis speaks on Igniting Change for asylum seekers – www.youtube.com/watch?v=93P3MrouAPU

Refugee story of girls Fariba and Fatima coming to Australia – www.youtube.com/watch?v=MlkMlpSQFO0

NOTE: **I was involved in meaningful community projects with recently arrived refugees as part of my PhD research**, which I wrote about, with my supervisor in: Morsillo, J & Fisher, A. (2009). "Appreciative inquiry with migrant youth for meaningful community projects." Book chapter in
M. F. Hindsworth and T. B. Lang (Eds). *Community participation and empowerment.* Nova Publishers.
Chapter online - https://groups.psychology.org.au/Assets/Files/Morsillo_19(1).pdf

MORE on asylum seekers page 56.

The Kindness Pandemic

By Dr Catherine Barrett & Celebrating Ageing

The Kindness Pandemic is an initiative of Celebrate Ageing Ltd, a charity combatting ageism and building respect for older people. It was established in March, 2020 by Dr Catherine Barrett in Melbourne, to support people doing it tough due to the COVID19 pandemic.

Dr Catherine Barrett's hope is that globally we will become a more connected and virtuous community, globally, in the wake of the pandemic. In tough times, when we are all in the same boat, struggling to overcome a common threat of a transmissible disease that can cause havoc in our world. Maybe we will reach out to each other in kindness more and care for our planet more.

We have seen signs of hope, in the ways our own government has responded with a level of kindness towards whose who are suffering during the pandemic. Whilst it may have been driven more for economic reasons, the outcome is still helping those in need more than usual.

During the pandemic local communities tended to connect more, getting to know each other better and support local businesses where they could, and appreciate nature more than we used to, with our daily exercise of walking and bike riding around the neighbourhood during lockdowns with limited travel.

Facebook pages for The Kindness Pandemic were created to offer a way to share local acts of kindness with others around the world, to promote kinder communities ,who care for each other and share what they have.

One story shared through The Kindness Pandemic page, was of a single mother in a supermarket paying for her groceries for small children, when she realised she did not have sufficient money. She cried. However, a few people in the queue behind her, handed over some notes to pay for all she needed for her children. She cried tears of gratitude for their acts of kindness.

The Kindness Pandemic - Facebook public group - www.facebook.com/groups/515507852491119/

Taking courage to share our kindness, to people and the planet, might be the key.

'Poetry, beauty, romance, love, these are what we stay alive for', this iconic Robin William's quote from Dead Poets Society, is a reminder to us that during times of crisis, it is caring for each other with kindness and love that helps us through tough times. Humanity can come together as one people to sing in unison, especially during a crisis.

Coronavirus might have led to people being restricted and isolated in their homes, however, art and culture is what connects people and brings them together during such times.

Italy found a novel way to keep positivity alive during the pandemic. People came out onto their balconies, each evening, to sing and play instruments, or to clap for the health workers caring for loved ones, as a way to embrace each other through the power of music. The streets might have been empty but the hearts of people in Italy were full of warmth and joy.

Shanoy, S. (2020). Five positive things amidst the Covid-19 outbreak that prove that the world is healing.
See: Curly Tales
https://curlytales.com/5-positive-things-amidst-covid-19-outbreak-that-prove-that-the-earth- is-healing/

The Kindness Revolution

by Prof Hugh Mackay AO, social psychologist

In the book, *The Kindness Revolution*, Dr Hugh Mackay explores how crises and catastrophes often turn out to be the making of us, connecting us and bringing out kindness for the best in the local community. He encourages us to find the best in ourselves and in our society.

For Hugh Mackay, to be kind always, and be kind to everyone, is to be fully, gloriously human. He says that every act of kindness is one more step towards a better society. He suggests that adversity can make us stronger, and pull us together more tightly, as a community.

Hugh Mackay encourages us to be **generous, optimistic and candid, so we can find the best in ourselves and in our society in both good and troubled times.**

He suggests that revolutions never start at the top. If we dare to dream of a more loving country – kinder, more compassionate, more cooperative, more respectful, more inclusive, more egalitarian, more harmonious, less cynical – than there's only one way to start turning that dream into a reality: each of us must live as if this is already that country.

Hugh Mackay reflects on the challenges we faced during bushfires and the pandemic, of upheaval and the questions many of us have asked. What really matters to me? Am I living the kind of life I want? What sort of society do I want us to become?

Pointing to our inspiring displays of kindness and consideration, our personal sacrifices for the common good and our heightened appreciation of the value of local neighbourhoods and communities, he asks in turn: 'Could we become renowned as a loving country, rather than simply a "lucky" one?'.

Mackay, H. (2021). *The kindness revolution: How we can restore hope, rebuild trust and inspire optimism.* Allen & Unwin.

Hugh Mackay's books – www.panmacmillan.com.au/?authors=hugh-mackay

Conversation with Hugh Mackay AO – www.youtube.com/watch?v=I5n206hhezc

NOTE on **Kindness of the Sikh community** during disasters

Sikh Volunteers Australia provides free, nutritious meals and essential items to those in need through their food van service, guided by Sikh values of compassion, equality, and selfless service.

Sikh Volunteers Australia – https://sikhvolunteersaustralia.org

Sikh charity delivers hope: Hot meals for flood-hit residents in Australia video – www.youtube.com/watch?v=SCfcX770_6k

Connecting with the neurodiverse & other-abled (othered)

We can become more aware of those in our community, who are *Othered*, because they face additions challenges, due to physical or mental differences, such as neurodiversity and people that are other-abled (considered disabled). As they continually face challenges, and they are always responding to and resisting the hardships they experience.

Consider connecting

Consider someone with a physical or social disability, surviving in this world, made for those who are mentally and physically very able. For example, so many public places with many steps to climb, or noisy spaces with no thought to dampening the noise level. Imagine dealing with this daily.

Now imagine this: "what if almost-all people could fly", but you knew that you could never fly like them [See website: www.thephilosophyman.com/blog/is-disability-in-the-body-or-in-society].

Some disabilities make life hard every day. But difficulties are made harder with our capitalistic and individualistic society. Yet, with extra thought and proper processes, we could make our communities more accessible physically with good architecture, and easier to dampen noise with good materials.

Consider connecting in action:

We can choose to walk alongside those who are Othered, when we can, like at cultural diversity events or other community events. Perhaps work alongside them, say: by donating, by promoting their programs and groups, by sharing their books and watching their movies, and by *'talking up their strengths'* in conversations.

Autobiographies by two prominent neurodiverse women:
Grace Tame: The ninth life of a diamond minor by Grace Tame (2022)
Australian of the Year 2021 – Grace under fire video - www.youtube.com/watch?v=KRcAWRPflOA
Ten steps to Nanette: A memoir situation by Hannah Gadsby, comedian (2022)
Video on three ideas by Hannah Gadsby – www.youtube.com/watch?v=87qLWFZManA

Celebrating Neuroadvantage

Dr Andrew Fuller, Clinical Psychologist

Andrew Fuller promotes kindness and celebration towards people who are neurodiverse. He challenges the traditional narrative surrounding neurodevelopmental variations such as ADHD, autism and dyslexia. Rather than viewing these conditions primarily as challenges to overcome, Andrew reframes neurodivergence as a collection of unique strengths and abilities that, when properly understood, can become powerful advantages.

Drawing from thousands of real-world cases, Andrew provides evidence-based strategies that help parents and educators identify and nurture the hidden talents within neurodivergent children. The book addresses common areas where neurodivergent children may face challenges – attention, sensory processing, reading, writing and emotional regulation – and reveals how these very same areas can become sources of exceptional capability.

Fuller, A. (2025) Neuroadvantage: The strength-based approach to neurodivergence. Amba Press.
https://ambapress.com.au/blogs/amba-press-blog/coming-soon-neuroadvantage-by-andrew-fuller?srsltid=AfmBOopPZeGUBralldZgA_tFAA1bxc6PoRSNnSaztrCnEG9zE41ssXlW

Mentoring young people

Fearless Women

Fearless Women is a group connecting with girls and young women in the ACT to help them to live life fearlessly.

They seeks to create a safe and inclusive community that encourages and equips girls and young women, to be who and what they want to be.

Some of the challenges they support young women through are: friendship issues, relationships, expectations to do well at school, body changes, and social media. All these factors can contribute to many girls and young women in the ACT feeling overwhelmed, stressed, and uncertain about their future.

Glenda, Fearless Women CEO; Dr Julie Morsillo; & Greta, Program Co-ordinator, Fearless Women

Fearless Women is a not-for-profit charity driven by a community drawn together with a common purpose. Using a gendered approach, the empowerment program provides mentorship, counselling and education services to enhance building confidence and resilience in girls and young women.

The team consists of our program staff, volunteers, and board of directors, committed to helping girls and young women in the ACT to be healthy productive and socially engaged.

Fearless Women website – https://fearlesswomen.org.au
Fearless women video – www.youtube.com/watch?v=CpLoeb2cQvA

Big Brothers Big Sisters of Australia

Big Brothers Big Sisters of Australia provides long-term, one-to-one mentoring to help change the course of vulnerable young peoples lives in Melbourne & Sydney.

Their vision is for vulnerable young people in Australia to have the opportunity to unlock their potential, creating a brighter future for themselves and their community.

This purpose is to provide vulnerable young people with strong and enduring, professionally supported one-to-one mentoring relationships, that change lives for the better, two people at a time.

They offer a diverse range of high-quality mentoring programs to meet the needs of young people across Australia. When a young person is referred to Big Brothers Big Sisters Australia, their qualified mentoring program teams assess the needs of the individual to determine which mentoring program is most appropriate.

Big Brothers Big Sisters of Australia
https://bigbrothersbigsisters.org.au/meet-the-team-who-we-are/about-us/
Big Brothers Big Sisters Australia video – www.youtube.com/watch?v=ewCDIEpAhz4

Mentoring Indigenous young women

Stars Foundation

Stars Foundation, a philanthropic trust, seeks to mentor and empower First Nations girls and young women across Australia, connecting with courage and kindness.

Stars provides a holistic program that supports Indigenous girls and young women to attend and remain engaged at school, complete Year 12 and move into work or further study.

The program is based on strong, trusting relationships. The Stars Room provides a culturally safe, warm environment. A place where the girls and young women feel nurtured and inspired.

Full-time mentors provide a diverse range of activities to support our Stars to develop the self-esteem, confidence and life skills they need to successfully participate in school and transition into a positive and independent future.

First Nations girls mentored by Stars have an outstanding success rate in Year 12 of 90-95%. In addition, more than 80% of Stars-mentored graduates are in further study or full-time employment two years later.

STARS OUTCOMES 2023

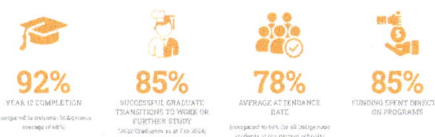

92% YEAR 12 COMPLETION (compared to non-Indigenous average of 86%)

85% SUCCESSFUL GRADUATE TRANSITIONS TO WORK OR FURTHER STUDY (2022 Graduates as at Feb 2024)

78% AVERAGE ATTENDANCE RATE (compared to 64% for all Indigenous students of our partner schools)

85% FUNDING SPENT DIRECTLY ON PROGRAMS

Stars Foundation – https://starsfoundation.org.au
Video of mentoring program – https://starsfoundation.org.au

Other Indigenous youth community programs for connections

Young Mob – First Nations youth program
www.worldvision.com.au/youngmob?srsltid=AfmBOorR0xfBV9pGVkDe5KKRUf2gLjsLuqZFHJ8MbpFlK8aO0qMqssFv

Victorian Aboriginal Child and Community Agency
www.vacca.org/page/services/youth-services-and-programs

NASCA – Culture, education Community
https://nasca.org.au – video https://nasca.org.au/why-nasca/

Koorie Youth Council
https://koorieyouthcouncil.org.au

> Love and charity, are service, helping others, serving others.
> There are many people who spend their lives in this way, in the service of others. When you forget yourself and think of others, this is love!
> Pope Francis (1936-2025)

Anti-bullying campaigns

Promoting kindness and respect, rather than bullying in schools and the wider community.

Bullying No Way in Australian schools

Bullying No Way is supporting Australian school communities with resources and activities for a proactive approach to bullying prevention and education. Resources on understanding, responding and preventing bullying are provided for young people themselves, for their families and for their schools.

The Australian Student Wellbeing Framework recommends five key principles as the basis for establishing safe and supportive school communities: leadership, inclusion, student voice, partnerships and support. Anti-bullying programs support these aims.

Bullying No Way - https://bullyingnoway.gov.au

How to deal with bullying video – www.youtube.com/watch?v=UX4AJhJfop4

Bully Zero – Cyber safety and resiliency programs

Bully Zero delivers face to face programs on cyber safety, bullying prevention, wellbeing and resilience throughout Australia. Programs are developed with experts: teachers, counsellors, social workers, psychologists, people with lived experience, and neuroscientists. The programs are designed to empower schools, community groups, sporting clubs and workplaces nationwide.

Bullying Zero – www.bullyzero.org.au

Kids helpline cyberbullying video – www.youtube.com/watch?v=ROHOSfH6Ess

Dolly's Dream – Anti-bullying programs

In 2018, Dolly Everett took her own life at just 14 after ongoing bullying and cyber bullying. You can donate to this charity, to help prevent another young life being lost and help give a voice to those silenced by bullying.

Dolly's Dream vital anti-bullying programs, include:
- A free, 24/7 Support Line available to those in need
- Anti-bullying workshops in schools, even the most remote areas
- Support services and resources for children, families, and communities
- Delivering programs free of charge to rural communities

These programs can help protect children and young people, and strengthen communities across Australia.

Dolly's dream - www.dollysdream.org.au/

Anti-bullying video by Dolly Everett's parents (2019) – www.youtube.com/watch?v=3sNuU9_6lmk

6 things Australia must do to tackle school bullying – https://theconversation.com/6-things-australia-must-do-if-its-serious-about-tackling-school-bullying-258924

Calls for gambling reform

Australians are the biggest gamblers in the world. Gamblers mostly loose money that could have been spent on the necessities of life for self and others, promoting a more caring and connected community.

Gambling is heavily promoted in Australia, with: large attractive casinos in many cities; lotteries in news agencies in each town, where many try to win millions weekly; in gambling on sports advertisements on television; poker machines in clubs; online games often looking like poker machines and much more. Australian will bet on anything. We have many problem gamblers.

The Alliance of Gambling Reform, is a national advocacy organisation fighting to reduce gambling harm and to give voice to those who have been impacted by gambling. You can join them to help end gambling harm.

>Australians are biggest gamblers - https://theconversation.com/the-biggest-losers-how-australians-became-the-worlds-most-enthusiastic-gamblers-252496
>
>Alliance for Gambling Reform - www.agr.org.au/

Gambling adversely affecting social cohesion
by Rev Tim Costello AO

Rev Tim Costello, has been named as a national treasure for his work as a pastor and lawyer, and community worker, including past CEO of World Vision. Tim remembers why he became the patron of the Anti-Gambling campaigners.

In 1992 he took on another female client; a married mother with three kids who ended up in prison for four years. She had never even had a traffic fine, but she had stolen $60,000 from her employer after developing an addiction to poker machines. This was a watershed moment for Tim Costello, as pokies had just been introduced in Victoria (before that Victorian's had to cross the border to NSW to use the pokies.) There were no protections or consumer warnings, and very little understanding of how addictive they were. *"I visited her in the women's prison, and I thought, how does a middle-aged woman with three kids, married, who's never had any trouble with crime in her life, end up in jail for four years? I've been fighting for pokies reform and gambling reform ever since."*

>Social cohesion is really fraying by Rev Tim Costello
>www.theguardian.com/lifeandstyle/2024/nov/23/rev-tim-costello-social-cohesion-is-really-fraying?CMP=Share_iOSApp_Other

Sports gambling in Australia

Australia already has the highest gambling losses in the world. Now, new data show that between 2015 and 2022, the number of Australian men involved in sports betting has increased substantially. For younger men, the rate of betting has surged more than 60%.

>Sports betting surged in Australia – https://theconversation.com/the-rate-of-sports-betting-has-surged-more-than-57-and-younger-people-are-betting-more-251902
>
>Grooming our children into gambling Equity mates video – www.youtube.com/watch?v=QA9iztjaxcA

Conceived plan to ease Australia's gambling problems

>Plan to ease Australia's gambling problems - by Charles Livington & Angela Rintoul (academics)
>https://theconversation.com/this-6-point-plan-can-ease-australias-gambling-problems-if-our-government-has-the-guts-256442

Supporting women prisoners

The Prison Network for women prisoners

The Prison Network offers connections by supporting women and children in and beyond prison in Victoria for nearly 80 years.

Many women in prison have suffered trauma and abuse which has been a driver to incarceration. Imprisonment, by its nature, is dehumanising, isolating, and intimidating. This can impact mental and physical health, diminish hope, and reduce capacity to create change.

In this space Prison Network aims to be a source of hope, dignity and purpose. They journey with women in and beyond prison, providing the support and courage they need to navigate positive pathways and create change. We help strengthen family and community ties and improve outcomes for children with a mother in prison. Through this relational support we see inter-generational cycles of incarceration and disadvantage forever disrupted.

Prison Network seeks to understand the complex interrelationship that exists between trauma exposure, disadvantage, and incarceration. Their approach is relational and trauma-informed, enabling women to find a way forward.

Incarceration can be a traumatic experience for many women who have already experienced significant hardships. The Prison Network delivers a range of in-prison programs that build a sense of hope, preconditions for change, reduce shame and stigma, and strengthen capacity for healthy relationships, including those with children.

Prison Network also delivers post-release programs. Women leaving prison encounter a range of challenges during their reintegration journey. The weight of stigma, diminished employment opportunities and the struggle to secure stable housing due to a criminal history, create significant challenges. The absence of robust support networks increases vulnerability and the potential continuation of prior experiences of domestic violence, further compound the challenges women confront.

Prison Network
www.prisonnetwork.org.au

OTHER programs to support women prisoners

Education programs for women in prison in Victoria
www.corrections.vic.gov.au/being-in-prison/programs/inside-out

Women prisoner support program in community in South Australia
www.abc.net.au/news/2025-04-03/support-for-women-transitioning-from-prison-to-community/105116836

Sisters Inside programs for women prisoners in Queensland
https://sistersinside.com.au/for-women/

Revive prison program for Aboriginal women in NSW
www.abc.net.au/news/2024-10-14/revive-prison-program-indigenous-women-back-to-work/104292262

Part 3: Advocate for universal human rights

N – We **need** to advocate for those without basic human rights: women, children and families in war-zones, those suffering injustice, abused or neglected, entrapped or enslaved. All peoples deserve basic human rights, such as: food security (healthy fresh affordable foods); free healthcare and free education; affordable housing and transport; meaningful work; time for creative hobbies; plenty of time for daily rest and recovery. Also, equity of income: no-one deserves more than the leader of the country (who is in turn accountable to others - not a dictator or billionaire wanting more).

PRACTICE

Hero – Former First Lady Eleanor Roosevelt, chair of the United Nations Human Rights Commission, driving force in creating the 1948 charter of liberties: The Universal Declaration of Human Rights.

Hero – Justice Judy Small on advocacy (2016) – psychologist, singer, activist and lawyer – speech www.youtube.com/watch?v=gJvopxOG0eE

> Sing out for justice
> (Justice Judy Small, 2016)

Human Rights poster by Zen Pencils
https://aungthan.com/store/humanrights

Human Rights ADVOCACY

Consider volunteering with a group that promotes human rights nationally and internationally. Check out:

- Australia Red Cross – www.redcross.org.au/about/
- Australian Volunteers (overseas) – Australian AID -www.australianvolunteers.com
- Amnesty International (Australia) – www.amnesty.org.au
- Anti-Slavery Australia https://antislavery.org.au
- Care Australia – www.care.org.au
- Common Ground (First Nations Australia) – www.commonground.org.au/about
- Foodbank Victoria – www.foodbank.org.au/?state=vic
- International Committee of the Red Cross (Australia) – www.icrc.org/en/where-we-work/australia
- Oxfam Australia (formally Community Aid Abroad) – www.oxfam.org.au
- Plan International Australia – sponsor a child - www.plan.org.au
- Smith Family – sponsor local child – www.thesmithfamily.com.au
- Tear Fund (Australia) – www.tearfund.org.au/what-we-do
- World Vision Australia – sponsor a child - www.worldvision.com.au

Humanities in Action – Australian Red Cross – www.youtube.com/watch?v=uW-LxohmGLU
Foodbank Victoria – www.youtube.com/watch?v=GojrttWxa7k
Australians are there – World Vision – www.youtube.com/watch?v=J72ashDO3qw

The **Human Rights Council** is an intergovernmental body within the United Nations system made up of 47 States responsible for the promotion and protection of all human rights around the globe.

United Nations Human Rights Council – www.ohchr.org/en/hrbodies/hrc/home
United Nations Refugee Agency Australia – www.unhcr.org/au/
United Nations Children's Fund Australia – www.unicef.org.au/

Consider: What disenfranchised group do I want to support, for them to have a better life with more human rights met? Children in poverty locally or internationally? Refugees fleeing war or abuse due to their race or beliefs? Indigenous children in remote areas needing education? Can you support with regular volunteer work or financial donations or join a peace march?

> You have to ACT as if it were possible
> to radically transform the world.
> And you have to do it all the time.
> *Angela Davis (1944 –)*

Human Rights PROMOTION

A. Join a peaceful protest march for peace (in war-torn countries) or for basic human rights for refugees or Indigenous peoples. While many are organised at the time and in the context of the situation being protested (keep your eye out for posters in your local area), there are also regular annual protests, such as:
   - Palm Sunday Walk for Justice & Peace – Faith Communities Council of Vic – https://vcc.org.au/palm-sunday-walk-for-justice-and-peace-2024/

B. Promote human rights and inclusiveness for local disadvantaged groups, by being involved with groups such as: Australian Human Rights Commission [https://humanrights.gov.au/our-work/] who advocate social justice for:
   - Aboriginal (Indigenous) peoples social justice
   - Aged discrimination
   - Asylum seekers & refugees
   - Business & human rights
   - Children's rights
   - Disability rights
   - LGBTIQ+
   - Race discrimination
   - Rights & freedoms
   - Sex Discrimination

C. Contribute to a human rights group addressing poverty or lack of education for Indigenous peoples, such as:
   - SNAICC – National Voice for Australian Indigenous children – https://www.snaicc.org.au
   - Koorie Curriculum (early childhood education for Australian Indigenous children) – https://kooricurriculum.com

D. Join a political party or advocacy group promoting human rights for vulnerable or the rights of the planet. such as:
   - Australian Greens Party – (greening planet & abolishing offshore detention) – https://greens.org.au
   - Human Rights Watch – Australian political parties stance on human rights – www.hrw.org/news/2016/06/21/australia-where-parties-stand-human-rights

E. Volunteer with a community group promoting **education** for vulnerable or migrants, like:
   - Teach English as a second language – in Australia or overseas or online – TEFL courses– www.tefl.org/en-us/about-us/
   - Tutor students struggling with school – Kumon Global (Australia) https://au.kumonglobal.com
   - Bridging program for refugees – Refugee Council of Australia – www.refugeecouncil.org.au/education-info/3/

Planner for Human Rights advocacy

International & national human rights	Local human rights volunteer	Contribute to human rights group	Join protest and/or political party
eg. ARC, Amnesty, Oxfam, World Vision, UNICEF, UNHCR	eg. Tutor in English for migrants or school children, learning for Indigenous children	eg. Sponsor a child a local child or in developing country	eg. Peace march, Indigenous Rights, Refugee march, Greens Party

Human Rights Values - Virtues in community

We need to value the human rights of others, as we need the support of others around us to survive. Modern evolutionary psychology, shows us that altruistic behaviour is crucial for group cohesion and consequently for the survival of the species. For instance, Prof Frans De Waal (2006) argued in his book, *Primates and philosophers: How morality evolved*, that human morality grows from our genes, and that the traits that define morality – empathy, reciprocity, reconciliation, and consolation – can be observed in many animals, most particularly in primates. According to Frans De Waal, empathy is an automatic response seen in dogs, apes, and human infants. It is an immediate response, arising too quickly to be under voluntary control. (Page 29)

De Waal, F. (2006). *Primates and philosophers: How morality evolved*. Princeton University Press
https://psycnet.apa.org/record/2006-20736-000

RIGHTS and RESPONSIBILITIES

You have the **right** to a safe environment
You have a **responsibility** not to abuse others

You have the **right** to voice your opinion
You have a **responsibility** to respect the opinions of others

You have the **right** to fair treatment
You have a **responsibility** to treat others fairly

Free Speech note

We all have a right to free speech, to have a voice, to have a vote, to offer an opinion. However, our speech should not hinder the rights of others, nor take away another's right to speak. Using *hate speech, threatening* or *belittling others*, or giving an opinion with no justification is not free speech. So, we have free speech, as long as our speech does not silence others, and it treats others with respect.

Freedom of Expression - Amnesty International
www.amnesty.org/en/what-we-do/freedom-of-expression/#:~:text=Freedom%20of%20speech,-Freedom%20of%20speech&text=While%20international%20law%20protects%20free,and%20incites%20discrimination%20or%20violence.

Whatever is currently happening with humanity, it is happening to us all. No matter how hidden the cruelty, no matter how far off the screams of pain and terror, we live in one world. **We are one people.**
Alice Walker (1944 –)

Human rights and our values

Prof Shalom Schwartz' theory of basic values

Prof Shalom Schwartz (2012) shows in extensive studies across 82 countries, culturally universal basic human values. He explains that "our values have been a central concept in the social sciences since their inception . . . Values have played an important role not only in sociology, but in psychology, anthropology, and related disciplines as well. Values are used to characterise cultural groups, societies, and individuals, to trace change over time, and to explain the motivational bases of attitudes and behaviour." (p.3).

Schwartz' introduction to his theory on basic values states that:
"When we think of our values, we think of what is important to us in life. Each of us holds numerous values (e.g. achievement, security, benevolence) with varying degrees of importance. A particular value may be very important to one person but unimportant to another. The value theory adopts a conception of values that specifies six main features, implicit in the writings of many theorists:

(1) **Values are beliefs** linked inextricably to affect. When values are activated, they become infused with feeling. People for whom independence is important value become aroused if their independence is threatened, despair when they are helpless to protect it, and happy when enjoying it.

(2) **Values refer to desirable goals** that motivate action. People for whom social order, justice, and helpfulness are important values are motivated to pursue these goals.

(3) **Values transcend specific actions and situations**. Obedience and honesty values, may be relevant in the workplace or school, or politics, with friends or strangers. This feature distinguishes values from norms and attitudes that usually refer to specific actions, objects, or situations.

(4) **Values serve as standards or criteria**. Values guide the selection or evaluation of actions, policies, people, and events. People decide what is good or bad, justified or illegitimate, worth doing or avoiding, based on possible consequences for their cherished values. But the impact of values in everyday decisions is rarely conscious. Values enter awareness when the actions or judgments one is considering have conflicting implications for different values one cherishes.

(5) **Values are ordered by importance** relative to one another. People's values form an ordered system of priorities that characterise them as individuals. Do they attribute more importance to achievement or justice, to novelty or tradition? This hierarchical feature also distinguishes values from norms and attitudes.

(6) **The *relative* importance of multiple values guides action**. Any attitude or behaviour typically has implications for more than one value. For example, attending church might express and promote tradition and conformity values at the expense of hedonism and stimulation values. The trade off among relevant, competing values guides attitudes and behaviours." (Schwartz, 2012, p. 3-4).

[Continued on the next page]

Schwartz, S. H. (2012). An overview of the Schwartz Theory of Basic Values. Online Readings in *Psychology and Culture*, 2(1). See online:
https://scholarworks.gvsu.edu/cgi/viewcontent.cgi?article=1116&context=orpc

Prof Shalom Schwartz' theory of basic values (continued)

The above are features of all values. What distinguishes one from another is the type of goal or motivation that it expresses. The values theory defines ten broad values according to the motivation that underlies each of them. Values influence action when they are relevant in the context and important to the actor. The ten broad values in relation to motivation are:

Self-Direction – Goal: independent thought and action--choosing, creating, exploring. Self-direction derives from needs for control, mastery and interactional requirements of autonomy and independence (creativity, freedom, choosing own goals, curious, independent) [self-respect, intelligent, privacy].

Stimulation – Goal: excitement, novelty, and challenge in life. Stimulation values derive from the organismic need for variety and stimulation in order to maintain an optimal, positive, rather than threatening, level of activation. This need probably relates to the needs underlying self-direction values (a varied life, an exciting life, daring).

Hedonism – Goal: pleasure or sensuous gratification for oneself. Hedonism values derive from organismic needs and the pleasure associated with satisfying them. Theorists from many disciplines mention hedonism (pleasure, enjoying life, self-indulgent).

Achievement – Goal: personal success through demonstrating competence according to social standards. Competent performance that generates resources is necessary for individuals to survive and for groups and institutions to reach their objectives. Achievement values emphasize demonstrating competence in terms of prevailing cultural standards, for social approval. (ambitious, successful, capable, influential) [intelligent, self-respect, social recognition].

Power – Goal: social status and prestige, control or dominance over people and resources. The functioning of social institutions requires some degree of status differentiation. To justify the dominance/ submission dimension, and to motivate group members to accept it, groups must treat power as a value. Power values may also be transformations of individual needs for dominance and control, such as: authority, wealth, social power [public image, social recognition] .

Security – Goal: safety, harmony, and stability of society, of relationships, and of self. Some security values serve primarily individual interests (e.g., clean), others wider group interests (e.g., national security). The goal of security for self or those with whom one identifies. (social order, family security, national security, clean, reciprocation of favours) [healthy, moderate, sense of belonging].

Conformity – Goal: restraint of actions, inclinations, and impulses likely to upset or harm others and violate social expectations or norms. Conformity values derive from the requirement that individuals inhibit inclinations that might disrupt and undermine smooth interaction and group functioning. As I define them, conformity values emphasize self-restraint in everyday interaction, usually with close others. (obedient, self-discipline, politeness, honouring parents and elders) [loyal, responsible]. [Continued on the next page]

Schwartz. S. H. (2012). An overview of the Schwartz Theory of Basic Values. Online Readings in *Psychology and Culture*, 2(1). See online:
https://scholarworks.gvsu.edu/cgi/viewcontent.cgi?article=1116&context=orpc

Prof Shalom Schwartz' theory of basic values (continued)

Tradition – Goal: respect, commitment, and acceptance of the customs and ideas that one's culture or religion provides. Groups everywhere develop practices, symbols, ideas, and beliefs that represent their shared experience and fate. They symbolize the group's solidarity, express its unique worth, and contribute to its survival. They often take the form of religious rites, beliefs, and norms of behaviour. (respect for tradition, humble, devout, accepting my portion in life) [moderate, spiritual life].

Tradition and conformity values share the goal of subordinating the self to socially imposed expectations. Conformity entails subordination to persons one frequently interacts—parents, teachers, and bosses. Tradition entails subordination to more abstract objects—religious and cultural customs and ideas. Conformity values exhort responsiveness to current, possibly changing expectations. Tradition values demand responsiveness to immutable expectations from the past.

Benevolence – Defining goal: preserving and enhancing the welfare of those with whom one is in frequent personal contact (the 'in-group'). Benevolence values derive from the basic requirement for smooth group functioning and from the organismic need for affiliation. Most critical are relations within the family and other primary groups. Benevolence values emphasize voluntary concern for others' welfare. (helpful, honest, forgiving, responsible, loyal, true friendship, mature love) [sense of belonging, meaning in life, a spiritual life]. Benevolence and conformity values both promote cooperative and supportive social relations. However, benevolence values provide an internalized motivational base for such behaviour. In contrast, conformity values promote cooperation in order to avoid negative outcomes for self. Both values may motivate the same helpful act, separately or together.

Universalism – Defining goal: understanding, appreciation, tolerance, and protection for the welfare of *all* people and for nature. This contrasts with the in-group focus of benevolence values. Universalism values derive from survival needs of individuals and groups. But people do not recognize these needs until they encounter others beyond the extended primary group and until they become aware of the scarcity of natural resources. People may then realize that failure to accept others who are different and treat them justly will lead to life-threatening strife. They may also realize that failure to protect the natural environment will lead to the destruction of the resources on which life depends. Universalism combines two subtypes of concern—for the welfare of those in the larger society and world and for nature (broadminded, social justice, equality, world at peace, world of beauty, unity with nature, wisdom, protecting the environment) [inner harmony, a spiritual life].

Interestingly: An early version of the value theory (Schwartz, 1992) raised the possibility that **spirituality** might constitute another near-universal value. The defining goal of spiritual values is meaning, coherence, and inner harmony through transcending everyday reality. If finding ultimate meaning is a basic human need, then spirituality might be a distinct value found in all societies. The value survey therefore included possible markers for spirituality, gleaned from widely varied sources (a spiritual life, meaning in life, inner harmony, detachment, unity with nature, accepting my portion in life, devout). However, spirituality did not demonstrate a consistent meaning across cultures. In the absence of a consistent cross-cultural meaning, spirituality was dropped from the theory despite its potential importance in many societies. [See more in online article].

Schwartz, S. H. (2012). An overview of the Schwartz Theory of Basic Values. *Psychology and Culture,* 2(1). See: https://scholarworks.gvsu.edu/cgi/viewcontent.cgi?article=1116&context=orpc

Universal human rights

A universal bill of rights was formulated by the international community, to remind us to respect the rights of each person and each culture, for world-peace.

United Nations Declaration of Human Rights, United Nations (1948), has 30 articles covering basic human rights, to encourage respect towards everyone, being kind to others, even those different to you. The declaration calls for freedom for all, and was developed after the genocide in Nazi Germany, and following colonialism with *'exterminate all the brutes'* (Lindqvist, 1996).

The Universal Declaration of Human Rights is a milestone document in the history of human rights. Drafted by representatives with different legal and cultural backgrounds from all regions of the world, the Declaration was proclaimed by the United Nations General Assembly in Paris on 10 December 1948, as a common standard of achievements for all peoples and nations.

It sets out, for the first time, fundamental human rights to be universally protected and it has been translated into over 500 languages. The UDHR is widely recognized as having inspired, and paved the way for, the adoption of more than seventy human rights treaties, applied today on a permanent basis at global and regional levels (all containing references to it in their preambles).

Signed by many countries, promoted by chair Elenor Roosevelt, First Lady of USA, after Nazi Germany genocide of Jews, Gypsies, gays & disabled - to make sure fascism never happened again.

www.un.org/en/about-us/universal-declaration-of-human-rights

Human rights include these areas of rights [see more detail over the page]:

- Right to freedom of movement
- Right to adequate healthcare
- Right to adequate shelter
- Right to adequate education
- Right to be treated with respect
- Right to meaningful work
- Right to time for leisure & rest
- Care of the earth for clean air & water
- Food and financial security

Australia is a party to seven core international **human rights treaties**

1. International Covenant on Civil and Political Rights (ICCPR)
2. International Covenant on Economic, Social and Cultural Rights (ICESCR)
3. International Covenant on the Elimination of All Forms of Racial Discrimination (CERD)
4. Convention on the elimination of All Forms of Discrimination against Women (CEDAW)
5. Convention again Torture & Other Cruel, Inhumane or Degrading Treatment or Punishment (CAT)
6. Convention on the Rights of the Child (CRC)
7. Convention on the Rights of Persons with Disabilities (CRPD).

www.ag.gov.au/rights-and-protections/human-rights-and-anti-discrimination/

Inspirational human rights for people and the planet, for us to sing about and enact.

Universal Declaration of Human Rights articles

This declaration was adopted and proclaimed by General Assembly resolution 217 A(III) of 10 December 1948. Preamble - Whereas recognition of the inherent dignity and of the equal and inalienable rights of all members of the human family is the foundation of freedom, justice and peace in the world. [See more preamble and more detail of articles - https://humanrights.gov.au/our-work/legal/universal-declaration-human-rights-human-rights-your-fingertips] Articles abbreviated:

Article 1	Right to equality
Article 2	Freedom from discrimination
Article 3	Right to life, liberty, personal security
Article 4	Freedom from slavery
Article 5	Freedom from torture and degrading treatment
Article 6	Right to recognition as a person before the law
Article 7	Right to equality before the law
Article 8	Right to remedy by competent tribunal
Article 9	Freedom from arbitrary arrest and exile
Article 10	Right to Fair Public Hearing
Article 11	Right to be Considered Innocent until Proven Guilty
Article 12	Freedom from interference with privacy, family, home and correspondence
Article 13	Right to free movement in and out of the country
Article 14	Right to asylum in other countries from persecution
Article 15	Right to a nationality and the freedom to change it
Article 16	Right to marriage and family
Article 17	Right to own property
Article 18	Freedom of belief and religion
Article 19	Freedom of opinion and information
Article 20	Right of peaceful assembly and association
Article 21	Right to participate in government and in free elections
Article 22	Right to social security
Article 23	Right to desirable work and to join trade unions
Article 24	Right to rest and leisure
Article 25	Right to adequate living standard
Article 26	Right to education
Article 27	Right to participate in the cultural life of community
Article 28	Right to a social order that articulates this document
Article 29	Community duties essential to free and full development
Article 30	Freedom from state or personal interference in the above rights

See: https://humanrights.gov.au/our-work/legal/universal-declaration-human-rights-human-rights-your-fingertips

Human rights and social justice advocacy in Australia

Human Rights & Social Justice
Human Rights and Social Justice address the fundamental rights and freedoms of individuals and the promotion of fairness and equality in society. Over time, the focus has expanded to include civil, political, economic, social, and cultural rights. It is crucial to recognise that human rights violations occur on both the individual and systemic levels and discrimination based on race, gender, sexuality, and socioeconomic status still exists, with marginalised communities continuing to be disproportionally impacted. Documentary Australia has documentaries on various human rights issues.

Documentary Australia - https://documentaryaustralia.com.au/issue-area/human-rights-social-justice/#:~:text=Human%20Rights%20and%20Social%20Justice,%2C%20social%2C%20and%20cultural%20rights.

Advocacy Australia
Every Australian has the right to the highest attainable standards of physical, emotional and mental health including to live and work in safe, healthy environments; the right to education; the right to life, liberty and security; to be treated humanely and with dignity; the right to freedom of thought, freedom of expression; the right to take part in the conduct of public affairs; to have equal access to public service; to have equal protection under the law; and, for victims of human rights abuse, the right to redress.

Advocacy Australia aims to advance social justice by increasing awareness of issues that impact the human rights of Australians. They promote and defend the human rights of individuals, children and families through public debate and where necessary, advocating for changes in law, policy and practice to address the fundamental rights of individuals experiencing suffering and distress due to misfortune and helplessness brought about by a lack of access, equity, rights or participation.

Advocacy Australia - https://advocacyaustralia.org.au/social-justice/

Justice and Equity Centre
The Justice and Equity Centre (formerly the Public Interest Advocacy Centre) is a leading independent law and policy centre, helping to build a fairer, stronger society by tackling injustice and inequality. Working with people experiencing disadvantage to expose discrimination and unfairness, using test cases and policy advocacy to drive law reform and systems change. The work protects and promotes human rights by challenging government and corporations, plus collaborating and partnering with others to develop solutions and achieve social justice.

The work combines: legal advice and representation, specialising in test cases and strategic casework; research, analysis and policy development; and advocacy for systems change and public interest outcomes through media, communications, submissions and engagement with decision-makers. Working across five focus areas: First Nations justice; disability rights; civil rights; homelessness and energy and water justice.

Justice and Equity Centre - https://jec.org.au
What are human rights? Video – www.youtube.com/watch?v=WJsUfck01Js

Human rights for Indigenous Australians

Colonial frontier wars & massacres

White Australian colonialists often would like to think that Australia has been a relatively peaceful country with no civil wars. However, that is far from reality. White settlers first came to Australia's shore in 1794. Over the next more than 100 years, more than 10,000 First Nations people were killed in Australia's frontier wars. Many thousands more died of diseases we brought.

Australia's Frontier Wars map - www.newcastle.edu.au/newsroom/featured/new-evidence-reveals-aboriginal-massacres-committed-on-extensive-scale

David Collins, Judge-Advocate of the colony, April 1789 - National Museum Australia www.nma.gov.au/defining-moments/resources/smallpox-epidemic

Genocide in Australia

The word "genocide" originates from the work of Polish lawyer Raphäel Lemkin who developed the term in 1942 in response to the Nazi policies of systematic murder of Jewish people during the Holocaust. Following the work of Lemkin, the United Nations Convention on the Prevention and Punishment of the Crime of Genocide in 1951 defined genocide as ANY of the following acts committed with intent to destroy, a national, ethnical, racial or religious group, as such: killing members of the group; causing serious bodily or mental harm to members of the group; deliberately inflicting on the group conditions of life calculated to bring about its physical destruction in whole or in part; imposing measures intended to prevent births within the group; forcibly transferring children of the group to another group.

First Nations Genocide in Australia - Australian Museum https://australian.museum/learn/first-nations/genocide-in-australia/

Deadly Story website - State Library of Victoria image - https://deadlystory.com/page/culture/history/Frontier_wars

Stolen Generation

The Stolen Generations refers to a period in Australia's history where Aboriginal children were removed from their families through government policies. This happened from the mid-1800s to the 1970s. The aim of this policy was to ensure the disappearance of Indigenous cultures and languages and to assimilate Indigenous Australians into the mainstream culture. This kind of policy was not limited to Australia and in fact South Africa apartheid system was based on the Queensland system This was part of the land and power grab that is colonisation! (https://meanjin.com.au/essays/emptiness/).

In the 1860s, Victoria became the first state to pass laws authorising Aboriginal children to be removed from their parents. Similar policies were later adopted by other states and territories – and by the federal government when it was established in the 1900s. For about a century, thousands of Aboriginal children were systematically taken from their families, communities and culture, many never to be returned. These children are known as the Stolen Generations survivors, or Stolen Children.

The Healing Foundation https://healingfoundation.org.au/who-are-the-stolen-generations/

Bringing them home report – stories of the stolen generations - https://bth.humanrights.gov.au

McGlade, H. (2013). *Our Greatest Challenge: Aboriginal children and human rights*. Aboriginal Studies Press.

Stolen generation song by Archie Roach – Took the children away – www.youtube.com/watch?v=IL_DBNkkcSE

Human rights for Indigenous peoples

Constitutional recognition

Indigenous voices have often been silenced by the colonising white people. Leaders of their communities are still calling for more meaningful recognition, such as in the book by leaders - *It's Our Country: Indigenous arguments for meaningful constitutional recognition and reform*. This is a collection of essays by Aboriginal and Torres Strait Islander thinkers and leaders

Australian Indigenous peoples suffered much discrimination and were not given the right to vote until 1962. Indigenous peoples were not counted in Australian census surveys until 1971. Also, many Indigenous peoples working on cattle-stations as drovers, farmhands and much more, were not paid proper wages. In theory they were paid low wages but, in reality, these wages were placed in trust funds and were never actually given to them at all. They just received food and shelter only, like slaves. The Australian government is now finally setting up some compensation schemes.

Davis, M., & Langton, M. (2016). *It's our country: Indigenous arguments for meaningful constitutional recognition and reform*. Melbourne University Publishing.

Stolen wages system – 1909-1969
https://towardstruth.org.au/themes/people/labour/52-stolen-wages/sub0464-stolen-wages-system

Indigenous workers stolen wages compensation scheme – www.theguardian.com/australia-news/article/2024/sep/06/nt-indigenous-worker-stolen-wages-class-action-pay-out-albanese-government

Australian Indigenous right to vote in 1962 – National Museum Australia
www.nma.gov.au/defining-moments/resources/indigenous-australians-right-to-vote

First Nations Peoples counted in census – National Museum Australia
https://digital-classroom.nma.gov.au/defining-moments/first-nations-peoples-counted-census#:~:text=In%201967%20Australians%20voted%20to.First%20Nations%20recognition%20and%20rights.

Racism

Racism towards Aboriginal peoples in Australia has been rife since white people first arrived. Starting in the early days of colonisation by British people with frontier wars, massacres, stolen generation, stolen wages with slavery conditions. But also ongoing every-day adverse racist treatment towards Aboriginal peoples in the communities in which they live, with bullying and even apartheid conditions. In the mid-60s, an Aboriginal university student, Charles Perkins, organised a bus ride with fellow students from Sydney into country towns in NSW to show how apartheid was working in Australia. They protested at public swimming pools where Aboriginal children and adults were not allowed to enter. This showed Australia and the world how badly we treated our Indigenous peoples.

Freedom Ride 1965 with Charles Perkins in New South Wales
https://deadlystory.com/page/culture/history/Students_lead_'Freedom_Rides'_through_segregated_NSW_towns#:~:text=The%201965%20Freedom%20Ride%20–%20led.New%20South%20Wales%20country%20towns.

Freedom Ride 1965 – Common Ground truth telling – www.commonground.org.au/article/1965-freedom-ride

NOTE: Calls for **'Closing the Gap'** for Aboriginal Australians – www.closingthegap.gov.au
What is closing the gap? Video – www.youtube.com/watch?v=cJSCLXBK0T8

National voice for our Children – SNAICC – www.snaicc.org.au -

Results of lack of human rights

Intergenerational trauma of Indigenous peoples

Indigenous peoples over the generations since colonisation by the British since 1788, have suffered untold trauma and misery, with the massacres, stolen generations and stolen wages (see previous pages). Plus, they have suffered from not being given ownership of their own lands, often not given proper housing, they didn't have a vote for so long, and suffered from discrimination and bullying, so many could not complete their education or be given worthwhile work with proper pay. They were silenced (see more next page). Many Indigenous peoples have become discouraged, some turning to alcohol to block out the pain, leading to more deaths from illnesses and suicide. Indigenous communities suffer extra grief with more young people dying than in other communities. This is intergenerational trauma.

Intergeneration trauma – Healing Foundation with videos – https://healingfoundation.org.au/intergenerational-trauma/

Incarcerated Indigenous Australians

An examination of the connection between relentless government intervention since colonisation to the trauma and disadvantage experienced by Indigenous Australians, have found that they are two key drivers of incarceration. Disproportionately high numbers of Australian Indigenous youth are in detention.

"We are imprisoning traumatised, developmentally comprised, and disadvantaged young people, where imprisonment itself adds to the re-traumatisation and complexity of supporting rehabilitation and recovery" (Milroy, 2021).

Incarceration Nation – Special Documentary, 1h 30m, 2021 – www.sbs.com.au/ondemand/tv-program/incarceration-nation/1930938947662

Commissioner Professor Helen Milroy – 2021 Australian of the Year – first Indigenous medical doctor
https://www.mentalhealthcommission.gov.au/news-media/news/commissioner-professor-helen-milroy-named-2021-australian-year

Indigenous Juvenile Detention – Creative Spirits
www.creativespirits.info/aboriginalculture/law/juvenile-detention

First Nations youth and the justice system – Transforming Indigenous health and wellbeing
https://timhwb.org.au/wp-content/uploads/2022/02/Stream-3_First-Nations-Youth-and-the-Justice-System-Fact-Sheet-_UWA.pdf

Indigenous **women are the fastest growing** population being **imprisoned** in Australia

First Nations women the faster growing group to be sent to prison, ABC News, 2024 – www.abc.net.au/news/2024-07-22/first-nations-women-fastest-growing-group-in-prison/104118174

Video on Indigenous women in prison – www.youtube.com/watch?v=P8k7YxqC_cl

[Indigenous women in prison program – see page 20]

Black deaths in custody

The numbers of Aboriginal deaths in custody have been so high that a Royal Commission into Deaths in Custody in 1980. The numbers are still very high with a public outcry in the community.

Aboriginal deaths in custody
News – www.abc.net.au/news/2025-05-30/aboriginal-deaths-in-custody-yuendemu-alice-springs/105354846
Report – https://humanrights.gov.au/our-work/publications/indigenous-deaths-custody-report-summary

Human rights for Indigenous Australians

Voice, truth and treaty.

Voice – Before colonisation, Aboriginal people had complete control over their own lives and were able to express their worldview and voice in language. Since 1788, their voices have been silenced and they have not had a say in their lives and in Australian democracy.

Treaty – One way that Aboriginal and Torres Strait Islander people have been fighting for self-determination is through treaty. A treaty is a binding agreement that is negotiated between different groups or parties, for example Aboriginal and Torres Strait Islander people and the Australian Government. A treaty is created to show that each group has reached an agreement about duties and responsibilities around sharing land and resources and governing together.

Truth telling – is about bringing to light our stories, histories and experiences and having them be publicly acknowledged.

Voice, Treaty, Truth –- Deadly Stories
https://deadlystory.com/page/culture/Annual_Days/NAIDOC_Week/NAIDOC_2019/Hey_you_Mob_it_s_NAIDOC_week

What is voice, treaty, truth? – Uluru Statement of the Heart - Indigenous Australians
www.youtube.com/watch?v=HZU7JyCs40Y

Uluru Statement of the Heart – https://ulurustatement.org/the-statement/view-the-statement/

Voice Referendum

In 2023 a referendum for constitutional recognition of Aboriginal and Torres Strait Islander people, was proposed: To alter the Constitution to recognise the First Peoples of Australia by establishing an Aboriginal and Torres Strait Islander Voice.

Australians where given a chance here to give a permanent voice to Indigenous peoples to give advice to government. However, fear and misinformation was instilled into people in the leadup to the referendum, which resulted in the referendum failing. This was a huge, missed opportunity to reconcile with the first peoples of Australia.

Failed Referendum Australian Human Rights Commission
https://humanrights.gov.au/about/news/opinions/year-our-voice-broke-fallout-failed-referendum-0

Why the voice failed – www.abc.net.au/news/2023-10-16/why-the-voice-failed/102978962

Truth-telling in Australia

Indigenous elders have been calling for formal public truth-telling processes, in order for Indigenous voices to be heard and for non-Indigenous to come to more understanding of their historical issues, leading to intergenerational trauma. Yoorrook Justice Commission is the first formal truth-telling process into historical and ongoing injustices experienced by First Peoples in Victoria, Australia.

Yoorrook Justice Commission for First Peoples of Victoria – https://yoorrookjusticecommission.org.au

Truth telling with Indigenous videos – https://yoorrookjusticecommission.org.au/videos/

'Genocide' with Australian Aboriginal youth incarceration rates by activist Dr Pat Dodson
www.theguardian.com/australia-news/2025/may/29/genocide-patrick-dodson-condemns-australias-aboriginal-youth-incarceration-rates

Local truth-telling in Australia – www.youtube.com/watch?v=_bjZ7xhk8Mk

Human rights for migrants

White Australia Policy
Historically, no Asians or islanders could become citizens of Australia from 1901 up until the 1960s and 1970s. But, from the 1850s many Chinese came for the Goldrush and often were the ones creating market gardens to feed the other new settlers also arriving, also enticed for the goldrush.

White Australia Policy 1901 - National Museum Australia
www.nma.gov.au/defining-moments/resources/white-australia-policy

Islander labourers
Pacific Islanders were brought in as slaves and later poorly paid workers to do hard physical work, like sugar cane cutting in QLD and fruit picking along the Murray River.

In 1863 a group of 67 South Sea Islanders were brought to Queensland to perform manual labour in the cotton and sugar industries.

They were the first of more than 62,000 Pacific Island men, women and children who were transported to Australia over the next 40 years. Some were kidnapped, or 'black-birded' (tricked or lured), others were misled.

Over the years, the Queensland Government attempted to curtail their exploitation but with limited success.

In 1901 the federal government passed the *Pacific Island Labourers Act*, which called for the deportation of most South Sea Islanders.

National Museum Australia Islander Labourers
www.nma.gov.au/defining-moments/resources/islander-labourers

Detention of Boat People
Asylum seekers and refugees coming by boat to Australia, often from refugee camps, having escaped war or violence against them due to their ethnicity, have been politicised in Australia, and been called illegal. Despite Australia having signed up to refugee conventions on human rights for people seeking asylum, giving them to right to find refuge in a safe country. Refugees coming by plane through a long process of migration are usually treated much better.

Detention of boat people - Refugee Council of Australia
www.refugeecouncil.org.au/detention/

ASRC policy on community-based processing
https://asrc.org.au/policies-old/community-based-processing/

Immigration is good for innovation in Australia – www.themigrationagency.com.au/why-immigration-is-good-for-innovation-in-australia/

Australian Government Immigration Strategy – https://immi.homeaffairs.gov.au/programs-subsite/migration-strategy/Documents/migration-strategy.pdf

Immigration is good for the economy video by Prof Robert Reich, USA – www.youtube.com/watch?v=LCl9-uaKzv8

Australia needs immigrants more than ever video – www.youtube.com/watch?v=eUgTERjlNgw

Displaced seeking sanctuary

Displaced seeking sanctuary from trauma

Today, more than ever in the history of humankind, vast communities of people have found themselves traumatically displaced from their home country, needing to seek refuge.

These displaced traumatised communities of people, often due to violent racial and ethnic discrimination towards minority and Indigenous communities, find themselves looking for a safe place of welcome and acceptance, of refuge and sanctuary. Somewhere they can find comfort and solace, to feel safe and at home, among people who offer them respect and dignity.

Historically and currently, people who have been displaced from their communities of origin, seek ways to find places of sanctuary. These places of sanctuary can include traditional sacred spaces and other public spaces that provide community and therapeutic services, to feel safe and to experience a sense of belonging, of community connectedness.

Sense of Community

We tend to seek a sense of community connectedness and belonging, where we are welcomed and safe, as a valued member of the group. David McMillan and David Chavis, building on the work of Seymour Sarason, defined a sense of community as "a feeling that members have of belonging, a feeling that members matter to one another and to the group, and a shared faith that members' needs will be met through their commitment to be together" (McMillan & Chavis, 1986, p. 9).

Their expanded model of a psychological sense of community has four dimensions:

1. *Membership* – a sense of belonging to the group, with a shared history and common symbols, that provides emotional safety for a sense of personal investment to be able to positively contribute as citizens of society

2. *Influence* – the development of trusting relationships for freedom of expression and empowerment

3. *Integration* – the fulfilment of the need for demonstrating competence to provide personal status with others who shared our values, as a protection from feelings of shame

4. *Shared connections* – the participation in, and sharing of, significant events for both negative and enhancing positive narratives of bonding

In a quest for a sense of community and safety, especially in times of disruption, people find themselves seeking places of sanctuary.

Sense of community by Dr David McMillan & Dr David Chavis
www.drdavidmcmillan.com/sense-of-community/sense-of-community-a-definition-and-theory

Building our nation: How migrants and their children have shaped Australia video – www.youtube.com/watch?v=xrLoqaPjU8c

Sponsor and welcome refugees into local communities video – www.youtube.com/watch?v=r2LB9gE6vto

Refugee Alternatives: Growing Australia's Role in Global Refugee Resettlement lecture – www.youtube.com/watch?app=desktop&v=X7hOxna4wFU

Place of sanctuary for displaced

Sanctuary, from the Latin root sanctum (sanctorum), is often defined as: a place of refuge; a place of asylum for people; or a sacred space with consecrated objects, such as a church, temple or mosque. But it has also come more generally to mean a hideaway: a room or other place where one can seek refuge from everyday concerns, a haven. It can also be a reserved area in which birds and other animals, especially wild animals, are protected from hunting or molestation.

A sanctuary, like a religious holy space or a wildlife reserve, is supposed to be a place of protection from harm for people or creatures escaping from harm.

Displaced persons needing sanctuary

Displaced persons can be persons physically molested and uprooted from their families and place of origin, or separated from family due by war, or some other trauma, dispute or wrongdoing.

Displaced persons are trying to find sanctuary, a place of refuge, both physical and emotional, where they will be treated with dignity and respect and welcomed into a community that respects and cares for them.

Convicts displaced to the end of the earth

There are many different reasons people been displaced from their communities of origin. For example, an ancestor of my family of origin, Jane Ison, was displaced from her community and country of origin, to be sent as a convict, enslaved to what seemed like the end of the world, where there was no sanctuary. Jane, desperate to survive in poverty-stricken England with no legitimate work available, she convinced a rich man that she would sleep with him, but when he undressed she stole his wallet. She was caught, and for her sins was deported to the other end of the earth on the ship Surprize (a surprise all right!) on the second fleet to the barren newly-formed British colony of Australia. Convicts deported to Australia had virtually no hope of ever returning to their families and homeland.

Indigenous people displaced from kin and country

Meanwhile, Indigenous people were removed from their traditional lands and ways of life, removed from family and kinship ties, and removed from their land with sacred places. These were heart-breaking times for Indigenous families who were displaced not only from their traditional roles as caring custodians of their country, for tens of thousands of years, but they also lost many of their children too (see more on previous pages).

It is a basic human need and human right to find safety and refugee, that provides us with a sense of community, a place to call home.

Morsillo, J. (2016) Seeking Sanctuary article in Academic (unpublished).
www.academia.edu/38189126/Seeking_Sanctuary

The Ukrainian refugees fleeing war and seeking asylum in Australia, ABC News video –
www.youtube.com/watch?v=cSoJsbz2sJQ

Refugee fears for safety in Papua New Guinea, ABC News video –
www.youtube.com/watch?v=bdssvfzskc0

Human rights for asylum seekers

Asylum Seeker Resource Centre (ASRC)

An independent service in Melbourne. The largest human rights organisation in Australia, providing sanctuary and support to people seeking asylum. The Centre has over 1,000 volunteers, and no government funding.

The Centre does the work that the government refuses to do for asylum seekers, who are refused the right to work, to access health, education or welfare services.

The Asylum Seeker Resource Centre offers:
- Advocacy – Legal aid, Detention advocacy, advocating from lived experience
- Empowerment – Education & training, employment pathways empowerment pathways
- Leap program – paid internships for asylum seekers for skills in program evaluation
- Food and material aid – Foodbank and community meals, ASRC Catering service
- Support Services – support, advocacy and referral services
- Healthcare – Health Centre with primary health services

ASRC https://asrc.org.au
Fadak's story – ASRC video – www.youtube.com/watch?v=yeKPZebgJ8k
See more on the ASRC in KINDNESS p.30.

ASRC Patron, Julian Burnside AO KC

Julian Burnside is a Patron of the ASRC, and has been named an Australian Living National Treasure (2004) by the National Trust of Australia (NSW). He is a veteran barrister who became a refugee rights advocate after working on the 2001 Tampa case in an action against the Australian government.

Julian Burnside speaks of the heartbreaking plight of refugees in a film on Border Politics called: *'Graveyard of dreams'.* The film documents the harsh treatment of asylum seekers by western democracies.

Burnside contemplates on how every life jacket left on a beach *"represents somebody's dreams of safety, of a better life",* and reflects on this grim place as *"a graveyard of a million dreams".* In the film you can see he was struggling to keep it together.

Offshore processing restarted in earnest in 2001 after the Tampa affair, when a Norwegian freighter rescued 433 asylum seekers from their sinking vessel, 140km from Christmas Island. Against international law, Australia refused the Tamp entry into its waters, sparking an international controversy.

Under, then Prime Minister John Howard the policy, dubbed the "Pacific Solution", saw all asylum seekers who arrived by boat intercepted at sea and sent straight to offshore camps established on Nauru and Papua New Guinea's Manus Island. Some asylum seekers still languish offshore.

Graveyard of Dreams video with Julian Burnside AOQC
www.theguardian.com/film/2018/may/03/graveyard-of-dreams-julian-burnside-on-the-heartbreaking-plight-of-refugees

Then I Came by Boat: Human Rights Arts Film Festival – www.theguardian.com/film/video/2015/jul/10/i-came-by-boat-hraff-audience-winner-asylum-refugee-vietnam-australia-video

Gendered human rights

Women's suffrage in Australia

Women's suffrage was achieved in Australia after decades of peaceful yet determined campaigning by thousands of women. The Commonwealth Franchise Act 1902 granted most (white) Australian men and women the right to vote and to stand in federal elections. Australia was the first nation in the world to grant (white) women these dual rights. Although, New Zealand were the very first to give women the vote in 1893 (but not to stand in Parliament). Enfranchisement promised progress, opportunity and self-determination. Proud of its achievement, Australia supported women's activists in other countries in their quest to follow Australia's radical example. However, Aboriginal and Torres Strait Islander women and men had to fight until 1962 to be granted the option to enrol and vote.

Women's Suffrage Movement in Australia – National Library of Australia
www.library.gov.au/learn/digital-classroom/feminism-australia/womens-suffrage
www.aph.gov.au/Visit_Parliament/Art/Stories_and_Histories/Womens_Suffrage_in_Australia

MeToo Movement

In 2006, the "Me Too." Movement was founded by survivor of abuse, and activist Tarana Burke. In those early years, a vision was developed to bring resources, support, and pathways to healing where none existed before. Working to build a community of advocates determined to interrupt sexual violence wherever it happens.

In 2017, the #metoo hashtag went viral and woke up the world to the magnitude of the problem of sexual violence. What had begun as local grassroots work became a global movement — seemingly overnight. Within a six-month span, the message reached a global community of survivors. Suddenly there were millions of people from all walks of life saying "me too". And they needed support.

Me too Movement – https://metoomvmt.org/get-to-know-us/history-inception/

Domestic violence against women

Violence against women is any act of gender-based violence that results in, or is likely to result in, physical, sexual or psychological harm or suffering to women, including threats of such acts, coercion or arbitrary deprivations of liberty, whether occurring in public or private life.

Around 95% of all victims of violence, whether women or men, experience violence from a male perpetrator. Violence or abuse is not always physical, such as: sexual, social, emotional, financial abuse, as well as controlling, coercive and intimidating behaviour.

United Nations Declaration on the Elimination of Violence against Women - https://whiteribbon.org.au/resources/

1800 Respect – National Domestic Family & Sexual Violence Counselling Service
https://1800respect.org.au/violence-and-abuse/domestic-and-family-violence#affectedbyDFV

Forced marriages

Forced marriages are still happening in Australia. Force, pressure and coercion should never exist in marriage. Forced marriage is a crime.

Life Without Barriers – support for forced marriage – www.lwb.org.au/services/forced-marriage-support/

Forced marriage in Australia & NZ report 2018– www.aic.gov.au/sites/default/files/2020-05/rr11.pdf

Forced marriage video by Australia Red Cross – www.youtube.com/watch?v=a2oXe0UDoSM

Human rights for disabled (other-abled)

Social model of disability

The social model of disability can be used to inform how to work, advance and promote the rights, health and wellbeing of people with disability.

The social model shows that 'disability' is **socially constructed**, rather than a medical model of a health condition, where people with disability are thought to be abnormal, different to what is 'normal'. 'Disability' is seen 'to be a problem of the individual to be fixed or cured.

The social model sees 'disability' as the result of the interaction between people living with impairments and an environment filled with physical, attitudinal, communication and social barriers. These barriers need to be changed to enable people living with impairments to participate in society on an equal basis with others.

The social model seeks to change society to accommodate people living with impairment, to support the right to be fully participating citizens on an equal basis with others.

The social model of disability is now the internationally recognised way to view and address 'disability'. The United Nations Convention on the Rights of Persons with Disabilities (CRPD) marks the official paradigm shift in attitudes towards people with disability and approaches to disability concerns.

Social model of disability – People with Disability Australia
https://pwd.org.au/resources/models-of-disability/#:~:text=The%20medical%20model%20of%20disability%20is%20all%20about%20what%20a,attitudinal%2C%20communication%20and%20social%20barriers.

National Disability Insurance Scheme (NDIS)

The NDIS is Australia's first national Scheme for people with disability. It provides funding directly to individuals. The NDIS provides funding to eligible people with disability to gain more time with family and friends, greater independence, access to new skills, jobs, or volunteering in their community, and an improved quality of life.

The NDIS also connects anyone with disability to services in their community, including: connections to doctors, community groups, sporting clubs, support groups, libraries and schools. It also provides information about what support is provided by each state and territory government.

The NDIS now supports over 500,000 Australians with disability to access the services and supports they need. This includes supporting approximately 80,000 children with developmental delay, ensuring they receive supports early so that they achieve the best outcomes throughout their lives.

National Disability Insurance Scheme – www.ndis.gov.au/understanding/what-ndis
Australian Federation of Disability Organisations
www.afdo.org.au/wp-content/uploads/2018/04/Medical-vs-Social-Model-of-Disability.pdf
What is NDIS? Video – www.youtube.com/watch?v=qZOjPBJiBPg

Dylan Alcott – activist, paralympian, Australian of the Year 2022
Cultural change around disability video – www.youtube.com/watch?v=2sVYVtxvH1g

Human rights for sexuality

Equality Australia

No one should be treated unfairly or subjected to harm and abuse because of who they are or who they love. To realise human rights in Australia, we need to end the deeply entrenched discrimination experienced by lesbian, gay, bisexual, transgender and intersex, queer, asexual and other sexually or gender diverse people.

Equality Australia grew from the campaign for marriage equality, led by the Human Rights Law Centre. They use legal, policy and communications expertise, backed by the people power of the community, to achieve equality for LGBTIQ+ people.

Equality Australia is building on the legacy of generations of leaders and activists who have enabled great leaps forward, as well as the strength and resilience of LGBTIQ+ communities. We need a fair and inclusive Australia for all LGBTIQ+ people, their families and communities.

Equality Australia – https://equalityaustralia.org.au
LGBTIQA+ glossary of common terms
https://aifs.gov.au/resources/resource-sheets/lgbtiqa-glossary-common-terms

History of Pride in Australia

1949 – Last repeal in Victoria of anti-homosexual *Buggery Act 1533* from England, criminalising sexual intercourse between men and man with animal.
1969 – Creation of Daughters of Bilites (later the Australasian Lesbian Movement) was created in the USA in 1955 and later moved to Australia to show support for women and homosexuals in 1969. The Homosexual Law Reform Society was also formed in this year.
1970 – Campaign Against Moral Persecution (C.A.M.P) was founded in Syndey and was the first openly-gay organisation within Australia.
1972 – murder of South Australian gay academic George Duncan by police officers sparked the call for reform within that state.
1975 – South Australia decriminalises homosexuality. First National Homosexual Conference in Melbourne University, supported by the Australian Union of Students.
1978 – Gay Solidarity Group formed with annual event formed in Sydney.
1994 – Homosexuality was decriminalised across Australia with the Human Rights (Sexual Conduct Act) 1994 (except Tasmania until 1997)
2013 – *Sex Discrimination Act 1984* was amended to introduce new protections from discrimination including: sexual orientation, gender identity and intersex status.
Dec 2017 – Same-sex marriage to become legal across Australia with the introduction of the plebiscite. This led to over 6,548 same-sex marriages being registered in 2018.

History of Pride in Australia – Out for Australia
www.outforaustralia.org/blog/a-history-of-pride-in-australia
Sydney Mardi Grac – ABC News video – www.youtube.com/watch?v=WBjtOCAnNCY

Note on **Adverse effects of pornography** on children and young people

The objectification of women in readily accessible pornography, with increasing levels of violence, not just erotica, is harmful to the impressionable young boys and girls who access it.

Adverse effects of pornography on children & youth
https://aifs.gov.au/research/research-snapshots/effects-pornography-children-and-young-people
Pornography is harming kids. Ho can we help? Video – www.youtube.com/watch?v=OzH7vslrETA

Human rights for slaves

Modern Slavery

According to Anti-Slavery Australia, slavery is more widespread than most of us would imagine. Sadly, the figures are:

- 49.6 million people live in slavery globally
- 71% are female (women & girls)
- Over 1,900 people in Australia are victims of modern slavery
- Only 1 in 5 victims are detected in Australia

Anti-slavery Australia

The community agency Anti-slavery Australia offers free legal services, research and advocacy for change, and training and advice to build capacity.

Anti-slavery Australia is dedicated to the abolition of modern slavery, including human trafficking, forced labour and forced marriage.

Their mission is to protect the human rights of trafficked and enslaved people through research, policy development, law reform, professional practice, education and advocacy. The core values that drive this organisation are: integrity, ethical engagement, excellence, accountability, professionalism and respect for human rights.

Anti-slavery Australia conducts research, working in partnership with other agencies, and undertakes commissioned work. The research areas include: modern slavery, human trafficking, forced marriage, dowry abuse, online sexual exploitation of children, asylum seeker exploitation, survivors' perspectives and modern slavery reporting requirements.

This specialist organisation works directly with victims of modern slavery as well as a range of community, government and industry partners, we are uniquely placed to provide advice and support on issues of victim identification, remediation and reparations.

Anti-Slavery Australia – https://antislavery.org.au

Historical Aboriginal & Islander Slavery

Australia's slavery started because other countries abolished it. Aboriginal people were blackbirded (tricked and kidnapped) and used in the pearling, sugar cane and cattle industries. They suffered terrible abuse and were denied their wages.

Many South Sea Islanders, 62,500 people, were blackbirded (tricked and kidnapped) from the 80 islands of Vanuatu and Solomons to NSW and QLD, starting in 1847, under the "indentured labour" trade to work in cotton fields and sugar cane farms. Around 30 per cent of arrivals died at the plantations due to exposure to European diseases, malnutrition and mistreatment.

Stolen Wages of Indigenous peoples
www.creativespirits.info/aboriginalculture/history/australia-has-a-history-of-aboriginal-slavery

Australia's hidden history of slavery – https://theconversation.com/australias-hidden-history-of-slavery-the-government-divides-to-conquer-86140

What is modern slavery? Australian Human Rights Institute – www.youtube.com/watch?v=82uQ8LzS9rk

Human right for basic income

Universal Basic Income

Money for nothing: is universal basic income about to transform society?
The concept of a guaranteed basic income might seem novel or neoteric, but it dates back to 1795, when the American founding father Thomas Paine suggested a "national fund" should pay every adult "rich or poor" a "ground rent" of £10 a year until the age of 50. Earth is "the common property of the human race", he argued, so everyone has been collectively dispossessed by "the introduction of the system of landed property" and was entitled to compensation.

Universal basic income would provide a vital safety net (especially with AI taking over so many jobs). "Under capitalism, you need money to survive. It's that simple," says Dr Neil Howard, an international development social protection researcher at the University of Bath. He and his team have helped to develop basic income pilots around the world and, like Thomas Paine, he believes that a redistribution of the privatised resources of all human beings is inherently just.

"The common wealth of the world and of humanity, should, by rights, belong to all of us," says Howard. "It has been appropriated by the few – and that leads the many to either have to struggle to survive or simply not effectively do so. So there's justice underpinning the claim of universal basic income."

Contrary to expectations, he says, "It wouldn't necessarily lead to people doing less work – it would enable them to do better work or to invest their time in more socially useful activities."

Universal Basic Income transforming society – www.theguardian.com/society/article/2024/jul/14/money-for-nothing-is-universal-basic-income-about-to-transform-society

Benefits of Universal Basic Income

This concept of Universal Basic Income (or Universal Wage) would save so much heartache for people who struggle to earn a basic wage due to different forms of discrimination and/or disability. A universal basic income would remove the stigma of being on welfare payments, and remove the need to stay in an unsafe household due to financial considerations.

Perhaps, polices could be formed, where no-one can earn more than the leader of the country in which they live. It could be hard to argue that any manager has more responsibility than a prime minister or a president or whatever of that country.

There could be policy changes to have disincentives, like taxes, for the owning of property that is not the home you live in. Plus, wealth tax and inheritance tax, and corporates and the ultra-rich taxed property, so that wealth in the community is a little more evenly distributed.#

Should we tax the rich? Research says yes. – Australian National University (2024)
https://cass.anu.edu.au/news/should-we-tax-rich-research-says-yes

Wealth Inequality & the tax system – The Australian Institute
https://australiainstitute.org.au/post/tax-system-turbocharging-wealth-inequality-in-australia/

Is universal basic income possible in Australia? – www.youtube.com/watch?v=GYFFhezswME

Global human rights & peacebuilding

Peacebuilding - United Nations & local human rights agencies

Our leaders need to listen to the community for their issues of concern, in relation to making peace with your past, so you can do more for the future.

The United Nations Association of Australia (UNAA) meets with heads of state and government, through the General Assembly of the UN, to take action to safeguard the future for present and coming generations.

In collaboration with the Initiative for Peacebuilding of Melbourne University and the Australian Institute of International Affairs (AIIA) to deliver regular summits and Future Roundtables. An annual Roundtable is often organised to discuss peace and security issues. In 2025 it will be the 80th anniversary of the Hiroshima atomic bombing. They meet, while clouds of war hang over Gaza, Ukraine, Sudan and Myanmar, to discuss the urgent need to revitalise the role of the United Nations in promoting international peace, development and respect for human rights.

United Nations Association of Australia – Peace and security
www.unaa.org.au/peace-and-security/

UN Peacebuilding – Peacebuilding Partners Australia
www.un.org/peacebuilding/Peacebuilding-Partners-Australia

Peacebuilding Initiative University of Melbourne
https://arts.unimelb.edu.au/peacebuilding

Initiative for Peacebuilding Uni of Melbourne video – www.youtube.com/watch?v=jann0ujaKGs

Psychologists for peace

Psychologists for Peace (PfP) are an Interest Group of the Australian Psychological Society. Its members are psychologists, and others, who are concerned about the prevalence of war and conflict in our world and are interested in applying their professional skills to issues relating to promoting peace and preventing war. They are working to promote peace in the world and prevent conflict through psychological research, education and advocacy.

Psychologists for Peace – https://groups.psychology.org.au/pfp/

Other peacebuilding and conciliation agencies

Conciliation Resources, Melbourne – www.c-r.org

Permanent Mission in Australia to the United Nations in New York
https://unny.mission.gov.au/unny/resources.html

United Nations Refugee Agency Australia – www.unhcr.org/au/

United Nations Children's Fund Australia – www.unicef.org.au

UNICEF for every child video – www.youtube.com/watch?v=E1xkXZs0cAQ

Building a secure future for Australian children video – www.youtube.com/watch?v=_XsH1zOItLA

Human rights - poverty and homelessness

Good Shepherd Australia & NZ - Youth homelessness service

Good Shepherd, aspires for all women, girls and families to be safe, strong and connected. They are committed to tackling the issues of our time which adversely affect them.

Good Shepherd is Australia's oldest charity working to support women and girls experiencing abuse and disadvantage. They provide services and support in the areas of family and domestic violence, financial insecurity and youth experiencing disadvantage.

Good Shepherd provides general support, information and case management to young people (16-24 years) experiencing or at **risk of homelessness.** They tailor the support to meet the particular needs of individuals and families so they can increase their independence and housing stability.

Good Shepherd Australia & NZ – https://goodshep.org.au/services/youth-homelessness-service-vic/
Melbourne City Mission Youth homelessness video – www.youtube.com/watch?v=CpvJetLq68U
Hope Street Youth & Family Services video – www.hopest.org/i-am-a-young-person/multimedia/127-homelessness-video
Australia's youth homelessness crisis – Behind the News – www.youtube.com/watch?v=tIPxpFyLf70

Micah Australia - addressing poverty

Micah empowers Australian Christians to advocate on the most urgent global justice issues facing our world today – extreme poverty, rising conflict and climate change.

Through our key initiatives and campaigns, we support Australian Christians and church leaders to engage our federal politicians warmly and relationally, leading to significant outcomes on key issues of global justice.

> To do justly
> Love mercy
> Walk humbly
> Micah 6:8

Micah Australia – www.micahaustralia.org/about-us/
Rev Tim Costello CEO – www.micahaustralia.org/news/author/tim-costello/
Why Australian AID matters – Micah Australia – www.youtube.com/watch?v=fP2ZtkGj1cI

NOTE: Adverse effects of **Artificial Intelligence (AI)**

Artificial Intelligence (AI) continues to evolve with little oversight, shifting the tides of poverty and power. AI can be defined as: *the theory and development of computer systems able to perform tasks that normally require human intelligence, such as visual perception, speech recognition, decision-making, and translation between languages.* The automation feature AI provides could replace an astronomical number of occupations.

AI is changing our future, but we have the power to shape how this might happen.
ABC News – www.abc.net.au/news/2025-03-02/ai-and-our-technological-future/104305614

AI power consumption in Australia
https://independentaustralia.net/business/business-display/ai-power-consumption-demands-a-rethink-for-energy-infrastructure,19513

AI regulation in Australia video – www.youtube.com/watch?v=cSzcWrm-qlY

AI is dangerous Ted Talk – www.youtube.com/watch?v=eXdVDhOGqoE

Local Community Empowerment Programs
to improve human rights

Big hART community program

Big hART programs are supporting young people to be confident and connected to their local communities through the arts.

The mission is based on the philosophy:'It's harder to hurt someone if you know their story'. The work sheds light on invisible stories, bringing hidden injustice into the mainstream. These stories make it harder to hurt someone, on an individual, community and policy level. The work demands best practise, striving for generational change.

Big hART was set up 32 years ago by Scott Rankin, as an innovative experiment to find new ways of dealing with disadvantage. Motivated by the closure of a paper mill in the industrial town of Burnie, Tasmania, Big hART began working with the community, creating high quality art to transmit their story. This began a journey that has taken the Big hART model to over 64 communities Australia-wide.

MAKE ART – Authentic, high-quality art made with communities.

Big hART brings virtuosic artists into communities to collaborate and create authentic stories which illuminate local injustice. These stories are presented to mainstream audiences to help raise awareness. This builds public support for change and helps to protect vulnerable people.

BUILD COMMUNITY – Everyone, everywhere has the right to thrive.

Big hART works with communities experiencing high levels of need. Rather than focusing on the problem, our unique non-welfare projects build on community assets, strengthening vulnerable individuals, and creating long term attitudinal shifts. The hope is for all communities to flourish.

DRIVE CHANGE - Positive, generational change begins as a cultural shift.

Big hART designs and delivers transformative projects to address complex social issues. The cultural approaches are evaluated and acknowledged as best practice. Decision makers seeking better solutions can use the award winning projects to help develop new and better policy. The aim is to drive generational change.

Big hART – Australia's leading arts and social change organisation – www.bighart.org

Scott Rankin, CEO & Creative Director – www.bighart.org/untangled-paths-by-scott-rankin/

Big hART Project Acoustic Life of Sheds – North coast of Tasmania project.
www.bighart.org/projects/acoustic-life-of-sheds/

Big hART Life of Boatsheds project video – www.youtube.com/watch?v=LqhfcFqnHzQ

Big hART Dance with Peace – Indigenous young women – www.youtube.com/watch?v=axfPLUv10bU

Big hART Tjaabi Project behind the scenes – www.youtube.com/watch?v=P8ZNXNz3jL0

Local community programs to improve human rights

Community agency programs to improve basic services

Anglicare Australia is one of the largest community support agencies for research and advocacy, with practical basic service programs and community development programs in each state of Australia. For example, Anglicare Victoria has programs in:

- Buldau Yioohgen (Big Dreams) youth support
- Community House – for isolated women
- Gamblers Help
- Homeless support
- Homework Clubs
- Mission House – emergency relief
- Prison support
- Victim Assistance programs

Anglicare Victoria – Community support programs
www.anglicarevic.org.au/our-services/community-support-programs/
Anglicare Australia – www.anglicare.asn.au

ASK IZZY – free service for basic needs

The Ask Izzy website, powered by Infoxchange, a not-for-profit social enterprise, has free community local help from anywhere in Australia. Ask Izzy website connects people in need with local housing, a meal, money help, support with violence at home, mental health and much more.

Ask Izzy – https://askizzy.org.au & video – www.youtube.com/watch?v=gCo5RzFwoAc

Community Hubs & Programs

Community hubs are embedded in primary schools and connect families from diverse cultural backgrounds with the wider community. They connect women and their young children with each other and their school through a variety of activities and with organisations that can provide health, education and settlement support

Community Hubs in schools – www.communityhubs.org.au
Community Hub in a school – Our Place – https://ourplace.org.au
Community Hub Grants – www.communitygrants.gov.au
What is a community hub? video – www.youtube.com/watch?v=v1GD2jRJ_18

Regional and community programs
www.infrastructure.gov.au/territories-regions-cities/regional-australia/regional-and-community-programs

Indigenous community development programs
www.niaa.gov.au/our-work/employment-and-economic-development/community-development-program-cdp#:~:text=CDP%20aims%20to%20support%20job,the%20CDP%20in%20two%20stages

First Nations approach to community development – www.youtube.com/watch?v=TJjkG4s1D4Y

Working with Indigenous communities' Ted Talk – www.youtube.com/watch?v=UKhVX1JF2n8

See more community agencies in:
KINDNESS ACTION & KINDNESS ACTIVIES

Human right of affordable healthcare

Australia has a policy of offering affordable or free health-care for all citizens, through a national healthcare system called Medicare. Emergency health-care in hospitals is provided for free, and public hospital beds covered, and some GP (General Practitioner) doctor visits covered by Medicare. However, it is a duel system, where those that can afford it, can get private health insurance to have more choice of specialist doctors and services, with less waiting time than those using the public Medicare only. Other countries have an national healthcare system, including: New Zealand, Canada, Taiwan, South Korea, Norway, Sweden, France, and Italy. Other countries have a hybrid system with some coverage for some citizens, including USA.

Australian government health-care system
www.health.gov.au/about-us/the-australian-health-system
Healthcare by countries – www.internationalinsurance.com/health/countries-free-healthcare.php

NOTE: The **World Health Organisation** (WHO) seeks to provide universal health care, especially in developing countries that do not have adequate or affordable healthcare systems.

WHO – www.who.int (recently USA withdrew support from WHO – see page 10.)

International community programs for better healthcare

Every human being has the right for good healthcare, that is free or at least affordable. However, many countries have little health care, which can particularly adversely affect women and their children. Some countries have little maternity support for women.

Birthing Kit Foundation

The Birthing Kit Foundation (Australia) is a humanitarian organisation that provides birthing kits and education in clean birthing practices to women birthing at home in remote regions of the developing world.

The Foundation works in partnership with the Australian community and a number of global organisations to pack and supply *Clean Birth Kits* to pregnant women living in rural communities and low-resource settings around the world. To date, 2.8 million Clean Birth Kits have been distributed to women in remote regions of over 30 countries, trained over 10,000 traditional birth attendants. Kits are given to mothers through community outreach programs, supplied to health facilities for use by doctors, midwives and nurses or distributed to traditional birthing attendants. They are designed to support hygienic practices and environments during childbirth in under-resourced settings. This has also contributed to the prevention of FGM (female genital mutilation)* in communities that are increasing the risk of death in childbirth.

Birthing Kit Foundation – www.bkfa.org.au; video – www.youtube.com/watch?v=umr1mcgLLK8

NOTE: Female Genital Mutilation

Female Genital Mutilation (FGM) can cause life-long physical and emotional harm

World Health Organisation - www.who.int/news-room/fact-sheets/detail/female-genital-mutilation
Aus - www.aihw.gov.au/reports/men-women/female-genital-mutilation-cutting-australia/contents/summary
Dirie, W., & Miller, C. (1998). Desert flower: The extraordinary journey of a desert nomad. Virago Press.
What is female genital mutilation? Video – www.youtube.com/watch?v=sIwQLgHHOZQ
The truth about FGM video – www.youtube.com/watch?v=WJwP6C5q6Qg

Human right for education

Everyone has the right to an education, preferably that is free or at least affordable. Australia, along with many other countries, provides a basically free education and compulsory secular education for to all children (from 1872) covering both a primary and secondary education usually over 12 years. Although, this often entails some cost for text books, uniforms and exclusions.

National Museum Australia
www.nma.gov.au/defining-moments/resources/free-education-introduced

Tertiary education was free in Australia for every course for a time (1973-1989). Whilst the government provides Commonwealth Supported Placements, cutting the cost of undergraduate degrees, overall tertiary education is becoming more expensive with students accumulating very large debts. This can adversely affect chances of buying a home, unless they have considerable support from wealthy families.

Student debt for tertiary education - www.abc.net.au/news/2023-07-27/generational-hecs-debt-university-access-higher-education-cost/102480290

International community programs for girls education

Education is a basic human right for all peoples. However, in some countries the education of girls has been discouraged or even banned. Some community groups work with locals in communities who have little education for girls, to support these girls and women.

Indigo Foundation - Education for Afghan girls

In Afghanistan, 1.4 million girls are still banned from school by de facto authorities, as all girls over the age of 12 are forbidden to attend public schools. This has been the case since the Taliban took over. Leaving Afghanistan as the only country in the world where secondary and higher education is strictly forbidden to girls and women. The international community needs to advocate to obtain the unconditional reopening of schools and universities to Afghan girls and women.

The Indigo Foundation in Australia, aims to improve education access and quality for around 10,000 boys and girls in a network of 50 education centres that include 40 primary and secondary schools and 10 local mosques in Afghanistan. As the Taliban have imposed significant restrictions on the education of girls and women including banning them from attending schools and universities after Grade 6, the Foundation are supporting the local Shura to continue to employ 10 female teachers in the local mosques to deliver informal education for around 300 girls in 2024/2025.

Education banned for girls in Afghanistan – www.bbc.com/news/articles/c36wyzl3n00o
https://indigofoundation.org

Australians investing in women - Afghanistan Education
www.aiiw.org.au/registered-projects/afghanistan-education/#:~:text=As%20the%20Taliban%20have%20imposed,for%20around%20300%20girls%20in

UNESCO – United Nations Educational, Scientific and Cultural Organisation
www.unesco.org/en/articles/afghanistan-14-million-girls-still-banned-school-de-facto-authorities

Fight for Afghan girls education video – www.youtube.com/watch?v=cZDhoxdkgcA

International community programs for early education

Dolly Parton's Imagination Library

Dolly Parton's Imagination Library is dedicated to inspiring a love of reading by gifting books free of charge to children from birth to age five, through funding shared by Dolly Parton and local community partners in the United States, Canada, United Kingdom, Republic of Ireland and Australia.

Inspired by her father's inability to read and write Dolly started her Imagination Library in 1995 for the children within her home county. Today, her program spans five countries and gifts millions of free books each month to children around the world.

"When I was growing up in the hills of East Tennessee, I knew my dreams would come true. I know there are children in your community with their own dreams. They dream of becoming a doctor or an inventor or a minister. Who knows, maybe there is a little girl whose dream is to be a writer and singer. The seeds of these dreams are often found in books and the seeds you help plant in your community can grow across the world."

By mailing high quality, age-appropriate books directly to their homes, she wanted children to be excited about books and to feel the magic that books can create. Moreover, she could ensure that every child would have books, regardless of their family's income.

This Imagination Library has reached Indigenous children in the outback town of Katherine, in the Central Desert of Australia.

Books for vulnerable young children to have dreams and education
A rich woman with a big heart – https://imaginationlibrary.com
Katherine Isolated Children's Services in partnership with Dolly' Imagination Library - https://imaginationlibrary.com/au/affiliate/KATHERINENT/
Dolly Parton's Imagination Library video – www.youtube.com/watch?v=fRyWw3od7Vo
Dolly Parton's inspiration video – www.youtube.com/watch?v=tscb01jfukc

Note on Adverse influence of advertising to children and teens

Children experience advertising in many forms, such as: TV, YouTube, apps, radio, billboards, magazines, movies, the internet, online games, text messages, social media and more. Advertising works on children, eg. the more TV a child watches, the more toys and junk food that child is likely to want and ask for. More recently, teenage boys are being targeted by *influencers* on social media to encourage them to disrespect women and girls, a form of misogamy.

Advertising influencing children and teens – Raising Children parenting website – https://raisingchildren.net.au/toddlers/play-learning/screen-time-media/advertising-children
Impacts of junk food advertising on children – ABC news video – www.youtube.com/watch?v=ea2t2Z1qMI0
Voices disrespecting women and girls (misogamy) – Respect – www.respect.gov.au/sites/default/files/2024-06/DSS_STOP2131_Factsheet%20A4_F_LR.pdf
Hidden trends of disrespect – Dept of Social Services – www.youtube.com/watch?v=-9ANHZzpT1o
Misogyny: origins of men's hatred of women in UK – www.youtube.com/watch?v=SPMOjevpQko
Andrew Tate's ideology driving sexual harassment and misogyny in Australian classrooms – ABC News – www.youtube.com/watch?v=VfC1HaAlaf8

Compassion as an act of resistance

As caring humans, following Jesus example, we need to reach out, in compassion, to those in need. As we like to be cared for in times of need, so we need to give that care to others who are in need. Those most in need can be refugees from war and now the environmental refugees from climate change.

We also need to care for our whole planet, as so many peoples of the planet will become environmental refugees. In 2024, there were over 122 million people who have been displaced, because of persecution, conflict, violence, human rights violations or events seriously disturbing public order, including over 1 million internally displaced in Gaza, and also environmental refugees [UNHCR video – www.unhcr.org/about-unhcr/overview/figures-glance].

As the young activist environmentalist Greta Thunberg said, 'I don't want your hope (or as some leaders are say, *offering prayers*), I want your action. If our house was falling apart our leaders wouldn't go on like we do today ... The extinction rate is up to 10,000 times faster than what is considered normal, with up to 200 species becoming extinct every single day. Erosion of fertile topsoil. Deforestation of the rainforest. Toxic air pollution, loss of insects and wildlife, acidification of our oceans – these are all disastrous trends," [Video with Greta Thunberg on climate change – www.youtube.com/watch?v=P0B6AxeVNY8]

"Some buildings are more than just buildings. But the Notre Dame will be rebuilt. I hope that its foundations will be strong. I hope that our foundations are even stronger. But I fear they are not. Around the year 2030, we will be in a position where we set off an irreversible chain reaction that will most likely lead to the end of our civilisation as we know it, That is unless in that time permanent and unprecedented changes in all aspects of society have taken place."

Greta is asking for Cathedral thinking, where we create strong foundations for our world, to protect and survive from climate change. Survival is not negotiable. The sea level is rising. We will have many more environmental refugees. Not just the flood islands either. But those in hunger due to over-heating causing droughts [Climate change linked to severe droughts – www.youtube.com/watch?v=8yJ0KXyk_50].

School children are asking for us to take this seriously. They want us to be compassionate about our planet and about their future existence. To make changes so we don't keep heading towards the destruction of our planet. Meanwhile, the rich want to continue on their way of using the fossil fuels and destroying our planet, so they may continue to become richer.

But we have been called to share our wealth. We have been called to forgive the debts of others. Forgiveness is not just about absolving wrongdoing. Instead, there is an old Jewish custom that Jesus also talked of. The custom of forgiving the debts of the poor who have borrowed from the rich. The poor who could not afford land and borrowed money, but were not able to pay it back. So, we too are called to share what we have, The resources we have, the land we have and the skills we have.

We are called to give hope to those in need. To be flower in the desert. But not just showing passive compassion, by being kind to those around us.

Although of course it is good to be kind to all. But also an active compassion, a compassion that resists the powerful and the greedy and those who do not care for vulnerable and do not care for the future of the planet. But just want wealth and satisfaction now.

Thankfully, we are a community that does care for the vulnerable, as Christ did. We do care for the refugees in our community. We do want our politicians to provide care and compassion to all refugees. We do want our politicians to provide care and compassion to the whole planet. So that we have a future for our children and grandchildren, and so that millions more are not displaced as environmental refugees.

Before Covid, I was asked to go to Cambodia to give some training to counsellors working with the poor there. Cambodia is one of the poorest countries in the world, due to suffering a genocide in the 1970s, where millions of people were killed and all were displaced from the cities and many starved. [Cambodian genocide video – https://study.com/academy/lesson/video/the-cambodian-genocide-summary-facts-statistics.html]

Thankfully, there are many inspiring people willing to show an active compassion for these people, resisting the powerful who say these poor people do not matter.

Australian missionaries, Ruth and David, are working in the slums, rescuing young men from the drug scene, giving them work to make t-shirts promoting messages of social justice, and insisting the men use there wages to go to school for education, so they can get out of poverty and support others for a better life. [Justees: Shirts for Justice – https://justees.org]

I met an Australian woman, Ruth, another Ruth who rescues girls from sex trafficking, providing them counselling, and teaching them how to cook creative cakes, yummy cup cakes and wedding cakes, to make and sell at her cafes, called Bloom Asia [Website & video – www.bloomasia.org].

A wonderful way to show compassion as an act of resistance. The people are so very poor, and the families sell their daughters into the sex trade, but this act of resistance, takes the girls away from the indignity, and gives them dignity. A creative skill that helps them feel good about themselves, making something beautiful and having a dignified survival skill.

I just want to end with a little local story of hope. Recently, for Easter Sunday, our Pastor asked me to hide some little chocolate Easter eggs for the children. His young daughter, was eager to join in. She was the first one to find an Easter egg. She proudly showed her find to her Mum. Her Mum congratulated her and suggested she look for more eggs. But Mummy, she said, holding up her one little Easter egg, I have my Easter egg. She was content with her one egg, with no greed for more than her fair share. But her Mum explained that she could collect more eggs to share with everyone. She was happy with that. This child showed compassion as an act of resistance. Like Jesus, who showed so much compassion to others who were in need, as an act of resistance.

> First they came for the socialists, and I did not speak out, because I am not a socialist Then they came for the . . . Then they came for me, and there was no-one left to speak for me. Pastor Martin Niemoller 1892 - 1984

Part 4: Challenge of greening the planet

G - Greening of the planet for sustainable life for generations to come is an imperative. Humans globally have been destroying the planet for our own ever growing needs and greed, causing climate change* Yet the natural world cares for us and gives us life, so we in turn must care for nature in sustainable ways. Our Indigenous communities in Australia and other parts of the world, have cared for nature and managed nature, so well for many millennia. We need action for our planet to sustain life, such as:

- Restore nature with more greening (& Greens policies)
- Sustainable food crops - permaculture, community gardens, organic farming
- Grow gardens and trees, reclaim forests and natural bush-land country
- Natural habitats for animals and plants, so less extinctions
- Water management for clean water
- Renewable energy, with light footprint on the earth
- Recycle and repair, cleanup of waste products
- Live sustainable lifestyles
- Consider *Small in beautiful*

United Nations Climate Change – www.un.org/en/climatechange/what-is-climate-change &
UN climate change – www.ohchr.org/en/stories/2025/05/right-here-right-now-global-dialogue-climate-change-and-human-rights

Climate Change Authority Australia – www.climatechangeauthority.gov.au

Challenge of extinctions – www.bushheritage.org.au/what-we-do/our-challenge/species-extinctions?srsltid=AfmBOooPVNx7LyrB8XbmPoMX5WX-61LGq279DulUAlGttZ4HKMDTWx_d

Water management in Australia (driest continent in the world)
www.nationalwatergrid.gov.au/about/water-in-australia

Small is beautiful book by EF Schumarcher (1973)
& Small is beautiful half a century on article in Practical Action
https://practicalaction.org/who-we-are/small-is-beautiful/

PRACTICE

Hero: Dr Jane Goodall DBE, Caring for the earth: Reasons for hope
lecture – https://kgl.com.my/caring-for-the-earth-reasons-for-hope/

Hero: Young Australian of the Year 2025 - Dr Katrina Wruck, Indigenous woman scientist
video - www.youtube.com/watch?v=zj2o4lxNNJ4

> Here we are, the most clever species ever to have lived.
> So how is it we can destroy the only planet we have?
> Jane Goodall (1934 –)

Greening the planet ACTIONS

A. Consider joining a group that promotes care of the planet. Check out:
- World Wildlife Foundation (WWF) Australia - https://wwf.org.au/about-us/
- Australia Conservation Foundation (ACF) – https://www.acf.org.au
- Friends of the Earth Australia – www.foe.org.au/who_we_are
- Greenpeace Australia Pacific – www.greenpeace.org.au/about-us/
- Australian Greens Party – https://greens.org.au

B. Get involved with an environmental group or environmental project
- Friends of the local park or river – www.foe.org.au
- Bushcare and Landcare volunteering – www.aabr.org.au/volunteering/bushcare-and-landcare-volunteering/
- Permaculture program – https://permacultureaustralia.org.au
- Transition town – https://transitionnetwork.org
- Eco-village – www.ecovillages.au

C. Think of ways to improve your local open public spaces working with local council and other locals
- More trees and plants
- More safe play equipment for children
- More areas for picnics
- More areas for local dog pets
- Improve wetlands or creeks

D. Start or join a community garden
- Own front garden or verge garden
- Local park or spare space for garden
- Join others wanting to start a community garden
- Planting fruit, vegies and herbs

E. Improve the natural environment in your own home and garden
- Indoor plants
- Colour in your garden – flowers & bushes - pots or in ground
- Food in your garden – fruit, veggies, herbs
- Little kitchen herb garden
- Tree and/or large bushes in garden
- *No plastic or toxic materials in the home*

Growing veggies and friendships – Gardening Australia video – www.youtube.com/watch?v=DTsGaaTbJ6o

Laneway Community Garden – Gardening Australia video – www.youtube.com/watch?v=n_fVs1k2b-Y

F. Learn more about an aspect of caring for the natural environment
- Permaculture – https://permacultureaustralia.org.au
- Indigenous plants & herbs
- Veggie & herb gardens
- Fruit gardens
- Flower & rock gardens
- Animal farming - dairy, beef, sheep, goats, pigs, chooks
- Crop farming - grains, veggies
- Indoor Plants

G. Find a local park to enjoy nature, walking regularly through the park

H. Visit a botanical garden with a walking tour to learn of local and Indigenous plants

I. Visit a zoo - be there for feeding time to learn more about the animals and their eating and survival behaviours

J. Visit an aquarium - learn more about sea creatures and what they can do

K. Make a conscious effort to recycle and repair – to reduce waste

L. Reduce use of plastics that often end up polluting our oceans

Birthplace of permaculture video – Urban Farming – Gardening Australia –
www.youtube.com/watch?v=Njucn01wv10

Planner for Greening action

Join group caring for the planet eg. WWF, ACF, Friends of the Earth, Greenpeace, Greens Party	Learn about environment eg. agriculture, permaculture, Indigenous plants, fruit, veggie & herb gardens	Improve local environment eg. Start or support community garden group, Friends of the park or river	Walking in local parks & gardens eg. Local parkland walks, botanical gardens, zoo, aquarium

Finding beauty in the world

I wrote this poem to remind me to appreciate the wonders of nature around me.

Look for the light, to light the way
Look to the sky, look at nature play

In the dark night of the soul, When all seems to be lost
Look up into the sky above, on a starry starry night
See twinkling little lights in the sky,
Constellations in the Milky Way

Julie in Kyoto, Japan, Dec 2024

In the morning, light comes in the sky, first rays of the sun appearing
Peeking above the distant horizon, brightening up the new day
Like a candle in the darkness, comes at the dawn of a brand new day

The clouds of dull grey doubt, still hover well within our sight
Sometimes they stay for a while, bringing the blustering storms of life
Blowing and pushing us along, raining all over our life parade

When the rain stops bucketing down, with the mud and slosh underfoot
A rainbow softly appears across the sky, reminding us life has more than clouds
Life has some colour, different colours, the soft hidden colours of the rainbow

When the sun comes back out, the first to greet a new day
Birds singing in the tree tops, chirping at the beauty of the sky
Chiming at the chicks of flying for food, to feed the mouths of hungry babes

Flowers start to open to the sun's rays, showing the beauty of the delicate petals
Letting out the sweet sweet perfume, for bees and bugs to pollinate
Savouring the nectar of the gods, bringing us colourful delights

Tall trees swaying in the breeze, telling tales of days gone by
Standing o protect with shade, breathing out oxygen all around
To give us the breath of life, to all creatures of the land

While the fish, many fish in the sea, keep swimming round and round in glee
Cleaning each other, feeding each other, keeping up the food chain for creatures
Providing abundant food for life to continue

Mother earth and sea are so alive, bringing us life, providing healthy life
Country of our ancestors of old, seas to quench our thirst each day
Life in abundance to be taken, if we can just graciously appreciate.

Appreciating the awe in nature

Phosphorescence by Dr Julia Baird

Dr Julia Baird, historian, journalist and nature lover, shows how we can experience transcendent moments appreciating the wonders of nature, in her book - *Phosphorescence: On awe, wonder and things that sustain you when the world goes dark,* by Julia Baird (2020). Julia writes of her youth:

"The beach there (Seal Rocks, few hours drive north of Sydney) was unspoiled, untamed, brimming with wildlife. We'd park (Julia and friends in their twenties) our cars and run into the Black Sea, diving and swirling under the moon, watching a silvery, sparkling ribbon of phosphorescence trail behind our limbs. The time sea creatures that absorbed the light of the sun were stirred up by our thrashing l; we were streaming sequins, or galaxies, in our wake. In truth they were phytoplankton that were reacting chemically to movement - generating energy from sunlight (photosynthesis) to drive light-producing chemical reactions when stirred up - but it seemed magical. These living lights became a kind of symbol of joy and abandon for me, and I tried to find more ways to experience them and companions who would love them as much as I did." (p.5.)

A beautiful, intimate and inspiring investigation into how we can find and nurture within ourselves that essential quality of internal happiness - the 'light within' that Julia Baird calls 'phosphorescence' - which will sustain us even through the darkest times. Julia suggests we: "Seek awe and nature daily... show kindness; practise grace; eschew vanity; be bold; embrace friends, family, faith and doubt, imperfection and mess; and live deliberately."

Baird, J. (2020) *Phosphorescence: On awe, wonder and things that sustain you when the world goes dark*. Harper-Collins Australia.

When nature becomes unbearably beautiful – ABC TV Compass with Julia Baird – www.youtube.com/watch?v=tJbotBgU9_w

Finding enchantment in the world around us

Enchantment is being captivated by the beautiful (not staying bogged down in daily problems and concerns)

Enchantment is the desire of the soul - thinking of our values, hopes and dreams

Enchantment is bound up with literature, art, philosophy and religion, psychology, sociology and culture - expressive ways to understand how to relate to others and the world.

Enchantment is art in its most charming forms, for moments of transcendence.

Enchantment can be found in religion, as in a guide for the perplexed (Jewish philosopher Maimonides) religion is a consolation, providing comfort of beliefs, ways of life and community. Religion or spirituality at its best can promote kindness and compassionate, a sense of social justice, to care for others, especially those in need and to do no harm.

The enchanted life by Sharon Blackie 2018 – https://sharonblackie.net/enchantment/

Blackie, S. (2018). The enchanted life: Unlocking the magic of the everyday. House of Anansi Press.

Nature trails for wellness video – Gardening Australia – www.youtube.com/watch?v=n9VaVU03jBI

Back to Nature documentary – ABC iView – https://hollyringland.com/back-to-nature

Promoting the wonders of nature

Darwin's wonders of nature

Charles Darwin was a biologist who wrote *The origin of species*, and other books, on the wonders of creation. He often has a bad name, in conservative circles, for his close study of nature and promoting the concept of evolution.

Interestingly, Darwin, also promoted the wonders of creation. He methodically explored the wonders of nature and wrote about the natural creation in his treatise (Darwin, 1958). He is probably the first person to write about nature in ways that are so readable, like a children's book. In fact, Darwin loved creation and he adored his wife and children, as seen in the movie Creation, and in the book: Darwin, his daughter, and human evolution, and Creation: the true story of Charles Darwin, by Randal Keynes (2002).

Darwin, C. (1859). *The Origin of Species.* John Murray.

Keynes, R. (2002). *Darwin, his daughter, and human evolution.* Riverhead Books.

McInerney, J. (2010). Review of "Creation," a film by Jon Amiel. *Genetics in Medicine* 12, 182–183.

Darwin's charms of nature

Levine offers a compelling interpretation of Darwin's works, evaluating their content and Darwin's prose style to identify a distinctly Darwinian attitude toward nature as a source of meaning and value.

Levine believes that Darwin exemplifies the capacity to feel "enchantment" about the natural world, suggesting that, if Darwin's example were followed, a "Darwinian re-enchantment of the world" would be brought about.

Levine identifies Darwin as a man who, charmed by what he found in nature—for instance, in his study of barnacles—finds community with every plant and animal, coming to love all living things, coming to feel what his place in the universe is: Quite literally, Levine suggests, Darwin loves you, just as he loves every other living thing.

Levine, G. (2008). *Darwin loves you: Natural selection and the re-enchantment of the world.* Princeton University.

Goldstein, A.M. (2009). The charms of nature: Darwin on meaning and value. *Evolution: Education & Outreach*, 2, 326–333.

The Enchanted Tree

A poem I wrote on appreciation of grand old trees, such as the Morton Bay Fig that my sister so loved and had in her garden.

The tree, a hundred years old, providing beauty,
life-giving oxygen, to living creatures.
A place to call home, for the birds of the air, to nest, to play.
A safe space for their young, with a community,
for other birds of a feather.
A place to sing a song of cheer to each other, like the Psalmist,
within the almighty encompassing arms, of the grand old tree.

Awe – appreciating the wonders of life

by Dacher Keltner (2003, 2023)

Prof Dacher Kelter describes *awe* as the upper reaches of pleasure and on the boundary of fear, yet it is a little studied emotion. Awe is felt about diverse events and objects, from waterfalls to childbirth to scenes of devastation. Awe is central to the experience of religion, politics, nature, and art.

Fleeting and rare, experiences of awe can change the course of a life in profound and permanent ways. Yet the field of emotion research is almost silent with respect to awe. Few emotion theorists consider awe in their taxonomies and those who do have done little to differentiate it from other states.

The Oxford English Dictionary cites that ``awe" is derived from related words in Old English and Old Norse that were used to express fear and dread, particularly towards a divine being. But as English developed, usage gradually began to suggest: "dread mingled with veneration, reverential or respectful fear; the attitude of a mind subdued to profound reverence in the presence of supreme authority, moral greatness or sublimity, or mysterious sacredness".

AWE for nature - People feel awe in response to large natural objects, such as mountains, vistas, storms, and oceans. People also feel awe in response to objects with infinite repetition, including fractals, waves, and patterns in nature.

Prof Dacher Kelter's research (Keltner, 2023, p.18) on the concept of 'awe' suggests that we find awe, in the eight wonders of life:

1. Moral beauty – *other people's courage, kindness, strength or overcoming*
2. Collective effervescence – *shared exultant feeling with a group*
3. Nature
4. Music
5. Visual design
6. Spirituality and religion
7. Life and death
8. Epiphany

(No mention of money or consumer purchases, or technology).

See more in his book, articles and videos (and more over the page).

Keltner, D. (2023) Awe: *The transformative power of everyday wonder.* Allen Lane, Penguin Books.

Keltner, D. & Haidt, J. (2003). Approaching awe, a moral, spiritual, and aesthetic emotion. *Cognition and Emotion*, 17:2, 297-314

Dacher Keltner: How awe will transform your life video – www.youtube.com/watch?v=q5WOWxfiqCQ

Awe by Dacher Keltner (continued) . . .

AWE in Sociology - Max Weber (1864-1920), a German sociologist and political economist, contends that in times of crisis people sometimes overthrow these stable forms of power, transferring their allegiance to a charismatic leader who awes the masses by performing miracles or acts of heroism. Weber's analysis illuminates how one charismatic person (such as: Buddha, Jesus, Joan of Arc, Gandhi, Hitler, King, Mandela) can stir the souls of thousands, inspiring awe and reprogramming them to take on heroic and self-sacrificing missions. [Weber, M. (1964). *The theory of social and economic organization.* Free Press.]

Emile Durkheim (1858-1917), a French sociologist, posited that certain collective emotions have transformative powers; they change people's attitudes and inspire them to follow something larger than themselves. Collective sentiments are triggered by stimuli that are associated with collective values (e.g., statements of ideological principles at a political rally), goals (e.g., rooting for the same sports team), and outcomes (e.g., suffering together through a natural disaster). Even the many natural elicitors of awe-like states, such as thunder, Durkheim suggested, are awe-inspiring because they have the potential of influencing the well-being and outcomes of whole groups. The elicitors of awe are vast in their meaning and effect. [Durkheim, E. (1964). *Essays on sociology and philosophy.* Harper & Row.]

AWE in Philosophy - The most systematic early treatment of an awe-like aesthetic emotion can be found in the Irish philosopher Edmund Burke's treatise on the sublime, first published in 1757. Burke defined the sublime as the feeling of expanded thought and greatness of mind that is produced by literature, poetry, painting, and viewing landscapes). Burke's treatment of the sublime advances our discussion of awe in two ways. [Burke, E. (2020) *Sublime and Beautiful.* Mint Editions.]

First, Burke theorised that two properties endow stimuli with the capacity to produce the sublime experience. The first is power. Burke writes: "In short, wherever we find strength, and in what light soever we look upon power, we shall all along observe the sublime the concomitant of terror."

Power, and in particular the power to destroy and control the perceiver's will, accounts for why certain entities are more evocative of the sublime experience than others (e.g., the bull as opposed to the ox). Power also accounts for differences between the sublime and another aesthetic pleasure, the experience of beauty."

There is a wide difference between admiration and love. The sublime, which is the cause of the former, always dwells on great objects, and terrible; the latter on small ones and pleasing; we submit to what we admire, but we love what submits to us" (Kelter & Haidt, 2003, p.301).

Keltner, D. & Haidt, J. (2003) Approaching awe, a moral, spiritual, and aesthetic emotion. *Cognition and Emotion,* 17:2, 297-314

How awe awakens and heals the brain video with Dacher Keltner & Jim Kwik – www.youtube.com/watch?v=nVAh5oBGoy0

AWE in Psychology

Charles Darwin (1809-1882), English biologist, analysed admiration, a close relative of awe. He defined admiration as a mixture of surprise, pleasure, and approval, as well as astonishment. [Darwin, C. (1872). *The expression of the emotions in man and animals*. John Murray.]

Abraham Maslow (1908-1970), American psychologist, is well known for his descriptions of *peak experiences*, which clearly involve awe. Based on his interviews with hundreds of people, Maslow listed 25 features of *peak experiences*, including: dis-orientation in space and time, ego transcendence and self-forgetfulness; a perception that the world is good, beautiful, and desirable; feeling passive, receptive, and humble; a sense that polarities and dichotomies have been transcended or resolved; and feelings of being lucky, fortunate, or graced. We will return to many of these themes in our analysis of awe, in particular the emphasis on the transformative effects of peak experiences. [Maslow, A. (1964). *Religions, values, and peak experiences*. Ohio State University Press.]

Across disciplines, theorists agree that awe involves being in the presence of something powerful, along with associated feelings of submission. Awe also involves a difficulty in comprehension, along with associated feelings of confusion, surprise, and wonder. We now propose a prototype approach to awe based on these two elements.

AWE: vastness, and accommodation.

Keltner and Haidt (2003) propose that two features form the heart of prototypical cases of awe: *vastness*, and *accommodation*. *Vastness* refers to anything that is experienced as being much larger than the self, or the self's ordinary level of experience or frame of reference. *Vastness* is often a matter of simple physical size, but it can also involve social size such as fame, authority, or prestige. Signs of *vastness* such as loud sounds or shaking ground, and symbolic markers of vast size such as a lavish office can also trigger the sense that one is in the presence of something vast. In most cases *vastness* and power are highly correlated, so we could have chosen to focus on power, but we have chosen the more perceptually oriented term *vastness* to capture the many aesthetic cases of awe in which power does not seem to be at work.

Keltner and Haidt (2003) further propose that prototypical awe involves a challenge to or negation of mental structures when they fail to make sense of an experience of something vast. Such experiences can be disorienting and even frightening, as in the cases of Arjuna and St. Paul, since they make the self feel small, powerless, and confused. They also often involve feelings of enlightenment and even rebirth, when mental structures expand to accommodate truths never before known. We stress that awe involves a need for accommodation, which may or may not be satisfied. The success of one's attempts at accommodation may partially explain why awe can be both terrifying (when one fails to understand) and enlightening (when one succeeds).

Keltner, D. (2023) Awe: *The transformative power of everyday wonder*. Allen Lane, Penguin Books.

Keltner, D. & Haidt, J. (2003) Approaching awe, a moral, spiritual, and aesthetic emotion. *Cognition and Emotion*, 17:2, 297-314

Basic Goodness and Awe: A Conversation between Tara Brach and Dacher Keltner – www.youtube.com/watch?v=r89JJdyO12o

Awe by Dacher Keltner (continued)

Prof Dacher Keltner (2023) proposes that five additional themes alter or *flavour* an emotional experience, giving rise to the variety and diversity of awe experiences:

1. **Threat** – Threat and danger cause an experience of awe to be flavoured by feelings of fear. Variation in whether an entity is threatening or not might account for how charismatic leaders (e.g., Hitler vs. Ghandi) or natural scenes (e.g., an electrical storm vs. a sunset) evoke awe-related experiences of dramatically different valence.

2. **Beauty** – Beautiful people and scenes can produce awe-related experiences that are flavoured with aesthetic pleasure.

3. **Ability** – Perceptions of exceptional ability, talent, and skill will flavour an experience with admiration in which the perceiver feels respect for the other person that is not based on dominance and submission within a hierarchy. Exceptional ability may often trigger a need for accommodation, but if there is no perception of vastness, then the experience should simply be labelled ``admiration'', not awe.

4. **Virtue** – People who display virtues or strength of character often trigger in other people a state that has been called *elevation*. *Elevation* is an emotional response to *moral beauty* or human goodness; it usually includes a warm and pleasant feeling in the chest and a desire to become a better person, or to lead a better life. *Elevation* appears to be a member of the family of awe-related states, but because experiences of elevation do not usually involve perceived vastness or power, they should be labelled as *elevation*, not awe.

5. **Supernatural causality** – Finally, the perception that God or some other supernatural entity is manifesting itself (e.g. seeing an angel or a ghost, or seeing an object levitate) will flavour an experience with an element of the uncanny. The uncanny is usually terrifying, but it can be glorious if the entity is perceived as benevolent.

Keltner, D. & Haidt, J. (2003) Approaching awe, a moral, spiritual, and aesthetic emotion. *Cognition and Emotion*, 17:2, 297-314

The thrilling new science of awe video by Dacher Keltner – www.youtube.com/watch?v=K-0JpJjPe74

Note on Rewilding to reconnect with nature

Wilderness queen Gina Chick, winner of ALONE Australia 2023 (67 days in winter wilderness in Tasmania), guides others deep into the world of rewilding, a growing movement in Australia, to discover ways to reconnect to nature, finding wild hearts and nourishing the soul while living in the city. Rewilding uses movements, meditation, emotional processing tools, ancient bushcraft skills and nature connection as transformative practices, dedicated to bringing people into harmony, with themselves, each other and our living planet.

Wild Heart Life programs with Gina Chick in NSW South Coast – www.wildheart.life

Alone Australia winner Gina Chick on finding our inner wildness – www.youtube.com/watch?v=ZeZ1_Xug0xI

Indigenous connection to Country

Indigenous communities have a deep connection to the Country, the land in which they and their kin were born. Indigenous peoples care for the land, as the land looks after them.

Aboriginal and Torres Strait Islander people are the oldest scientists in human history. They have prospered here in Australia for 65,000 years or more. Many First Peoples regard the land as a reflection of the sky and the sky a reflection of the land. Sophisticated astronomical expertise embedded within the Dreaming and Songlines is interwoven into a deep understanding of changes on the land, such as weather patterns and seasonal shifts, that are integral to knowledges of time, food availability, and ceremony. The First Knowledges series provides a deeper understanding of the expertise and ingenuity of Indigenous Australians.

First knowledges collection - https://antar.org.au/shop/the-first-knowledges-series/
Noon, K. (2022). *Astronomy: Sky Country* (K. De Napoli, Ed.) in First Knowledges Collection. Thames & Hudson Australia.

Indigenous land management in Australia - www.agriculture.gov.au/sites/default/files/sitecollectiondocuments/natural-resources/landcare/submissions/ilm-factsheet.pdf

Caring for our country benefits - https://aiatsis.gov.au/sites/default/files/research_pub/benefits-cfc_0_3.

Indigenous Spirituality & theology
Callaghan, P., & Gordon, P. (2022). *The dreaming path: Indigenous thinking to change your life*. Pantera Press
Deverell, G. W., & Pattel-Gray, A. (2023). *Contemplating country: More Gondwana theology*. Wipf & Stock.

Nature as healer

Indigenous peoples have a very long history of understanding the healing powers of nature. In Western cultures, there has been a tradition to view nature as *healer* in various ways, such as, a garden for the ill first appears in Europe during the Middle Ages, with monastic hospitals providing enclosed vegetation gardens with an earnest wish for the spiritual transformation of patients. The therapeutic effects of nature to improve patients' recovery has been, for the first time, precisely written and published by Florence Nightingale in Notes on Nursing in 1860. She believed that visual connections to nature, such as natural scenes through window and bedside flowers, aided the recovery of patients (Jiang, 2013).

Indigenous healing programs – The Healing Foundation
https://healingfoundation.org.au/app/uploads/2017/02/Aboriginal-and-Torres-Strait-Islander-Healing-Programs-A-Literature-Review.pdf

Sharing two world views of nature's healing – www.metaphoricallyspeaking.com.au/two-world-views/

Jiang, S. (2013). Therapeutic landscapes and healing gardens: A review of Chinese literature in relation to the studies in Western countries. *Frontiers of Architectural Research* (2014) 3, p. 141-153.

Nature Based Therapy – www.naturebasedtherapy.com.au – *See more in previous handbook*

What is Indigenous land management? Video – www.youtube.com/watch?v=PiQCI329TBY

Desserts to gardens: Indigenous land management techniques - www.youtube.com/watch?v=5u9s8m8uaO4

Environmental Psychology

by Dr Susie Burke, environmental psychologist.

Dr Susie Burke with much consultation, has developed an empowering handbook for the Australian Psychological Society, on psychological strategies to tackle climate change that is adversely affecting our planet (Burke, 2017).

She has developed these eight insights, making the acronym ACTIVATE, in the hope they will ACTIVATE the public into more effectively engaging with the challenge of climate change:

1. Acknowledge feelings about climate change to yourself and others and learn ways of managing feelings so you can face and not avoid the reality of climate change.

2. Create social norms about protecting the environment so that people see that 'everyone is doing it' and 'it's normal to be green'.

3. Talk about climate change and break the collective silence so that more and more people see it as a risk that requires action

4. Inspire positive visions of a low-energy, sustainable, zero carbon world so that people know what we are working towards and can identify steps to get there.

5. Value it – show people how their core values are often linked to other values that are about restoring a safe climate, and that caring about these issues actually reinforces their core values.

6. Act personally and collectively to contribute to climate change solutions and feel engaged and less despairing.

7. Time is now. Show people that climate change is here, now and for sure so they see it is timely and relevant to them and impacts the things that they care deeply about.

8. Engage with nature to restore your spirits and connect with the very places that you are trying to protect.

Burke, S. (2017) The climate change empowerment handbook: Psychological strategies to tackle climate change. Australian Psychological Society.

Handbook available online: https://psychology.org.au/getmedia/88ee1716-2604-44ce-b87a-ca0408dfaa12/climate-change-empowerment-handbook.pdf

Susie Burke Psychology website: www.susieburke.com.au
Susie Burke on psychology of climate change video - www.youtube.com/watch?v=9yBWfwN3wwY

Psychological first aid after disasters AIPC video – www.youtube.com/watch?v=FMbmu07cA6k

Eco-anxiety – Australin Youth Climate Coalition video – www.youtube.com/watch?v=XgTBhFxL70c

The space between hope and despair
by Dr Susie Burke

Dr Susie Burke speaks of the need for hope in the face of life's challenges, including concern for the adverse effects of climate change:

"Hope comes in myriad forms, each one the catalyst for a different response, and some more useful than others. Ask yourself, what hope do you have?

Cultivating hope is an example of what psychologists call *meaning focused coping strategies*, where the meanings that we attribute to climate change can help us to stay engaged with the problem, as well as helping us to manage the difficult feelings.

The concept of hope always turns up when the going gets tough, whether we're dealing with personal challenges like illness or great loss, or enormous societal challenges like climate change. We wonder if there's *any hope*, or if it's *hopeless*, or whether we're just *indulging false hopes*.

We get that hope is a good thing to have, and that having no hope is pretty miserable, but why is hope useful, and what exactly is it (it's a very abstract noun), and how can we cultivate hope on something like climate change without just being naïve, or underestimating the severity of the problem, or *brightsiding?*

Hope is an integral part of being human. It's what gets us out of bed each day and gives us the reason to go on when faced with adversity, trials and threats. Social scientists like psychologists have found it to be a contributing factor in helping people recover from disasters, illness, trauma, and tragedy. Hope is one of the five key elements that we promote in psychological first aid, and in helping people recover from floods, cyclones, bushfires and other natural disasters.

Without hope we risk becoming depressed. There is a considerable body of research looking at the relationship between being depressed and hopeless. Being depressed isn't good for anyone. (Unless, as George Monbiot quips in his introduction to Heat, you get so depressed that you go to bed and pull the covers over your head and stay put – thereby drastically reducing your carbon footprint burn fewer fossil fuels in the process).

Without hope, we also risk resigning ourselves to disaster, focusing only on adaptation and no longer putting efforts into mitigation. Without hope, some will turn towards nihilism, we risk people deciding to just enjoy the riches of fossil fuels and no longer making efforts. So, what type of hope is most helpful?"

Burke, S. (2020). The space between hope and despair. *Dumb Feather* article 13 January, 2020. www.dumbofeather.com/articles/the-space-between-hope-and-despair/

Mental Health First Aid Australia video – www.youtube.com/watch?v=qJgbyZQaO1c

Activists caring for nature

Climate Activists Network Australia

Climate Action Network Australia (CANA) is a network of organisations working together to protect people from climate change and its impacts, to safeguard our natural environment, and to build a fairer and healthier Australia for everyone. Here you can find a group to join, with shared values, people of your tribe.

Climate Activists Network Australia – www.cana.net.au/ourwork

Australian teen takes on government over climate harm video – www.youtube.com/watch?v=fhmGkJDtLtU

Bob Brown Foundation

In the age of rapid destruction of the biosphere, attended by cynicism and pessimism, the Bob Brown Foundation uses ecological reality and optimism to promote real environmental wins. They are committed to defending wild places and wildlife.

The Foundation is funded by the generosity of people. Support powers the campaigns to protect wild nature and take action for earth.

Bob Brown Foundation – https://bobbrown.org.au

Take action to stop extinction with Bob Bronw video – www.youtube.com/watch?v=wzCZtHZ6LAQ

Australian Youth Climate Coalition

Australian youth building a generation-wide movement of young people leading solutions to the climate crisis, by shifting the power for a clean and just future.

Working for a future grounded in climate justice, where people on the frontlines of climate change can take back power and lead solutions from the ground up.

Australian Youth Climate Coalition – www.aycc.org.au

Australian Youth Climate Coalition Dirrum Festival – www.youtube.com/watch?v=B2J2VM9ChUA

Parents for Climate

Parents for Climate, which facilitates meetings with like-minded parents, and takes actions such as writing to state and federal members of parliament.

Be brave, stay positive and find your tribe – Parents for Change
www.theguardian.com/australia-news/2024/feb/17/be-brave-stay-positive-find-your-tribe-three-climate-activists-explain-how-to-get-started

Regenerators

The Regenerators is a platform created by Regen Studios - an Australian based film and impact production company dedicated to producing and amplifying screen content that informs, inspires and activates audiences.

Regenerators video - https://theregenerators.org/2040/

What is Australia doing about climate change? Video – www.youtube.com/watch?v=cJiCRi6oJSg

Earth's seasonal rhythms are changing putting systems at risk – www.ndtv.com/world-news/earths-seasonal-rhythms-are-changing-putting-species-and-ecosystems-at-risk-8547511

Adapting to climate change – https://theconversation.com/adapting-to-climate-change-is-limited-by-peoples-behaviour-how-social-innovation-can-help-247374

Global activists David Attenborough & Greta Thunberg

Caring for the planet and caring for the local natural community environment, by thinking globally, and acting locally to care for all creation can be good for the soul and the planet that sustains us. Today, our young people (like Greta Thunberg), and our scientists (like David Attenborough) are calling us to us care for our world, before we destroy it. For them, a virtuous community is one that cares for the planet first, so we have a safe and clean and healthy place to live, so we can have a virtuous community that is kind and compassionate to each other. If we learn to be kind to the natural environment, to all creatures of the earth, and the people in need in our community, including environmental refugees, then we will have a virtuous community.

Interview David Attenborough with Greta Thunberg.
https://youtu.be/-pP7M20iNsc

A life on our planet: My witness statement and a vision for the future

David Attenborough, award-winning broadcaster and natural historian, gives a scientifically informed account of the changes occurring in the world over the last century, sharing a lifetime of wisdom and a hopeful vision for the future. At 93 years old, David Attenborough stated: "I've had an extraordinary life. It's only now that I appreciate how extraordinary. As a young man, I felt I was out there in the wild, experiencing the untouched natural world – but it was an illusion. The tragedy of our time has been happening all around us, barely noticeable from day to day -- the loss of our planet's wild places, its biodiversity. I have been witness to this decline."

A Life on Our Planet is his witness statement, and vision for the future. It is the story of how we came to make this, our greatest mistake -- and how, if we act now, we can yet put it right. We have one final chance to create the perfect home for ourselves and restore the wonderful world we inherited. All we need is the will to do so"—

No One Is Too Small to Make a Difference is a book by climate activist Greta Thunberg. It was published on 30 May 2019. It consists of a collection of eleven speeches which she has written and presented about global warming and the climate crisis.

Attenborough, D. (2021). *A life on our planet: My witness statement and a vision for the future*. Penguin Books

Thunberg, G. (2019). *No one is too small to make a difference.* Random House.

Scientist explains how climate crisis would be averted video by Greta Thunberg – https://www.youtube.com/watch?v=bkrcxLgHn-w

A perfect planet documentary by David Denborough – BBC - www.youtube.com/watch?v=7MxeAPR-uvQ&list=PLz58QJ68R9CTFoR1J6dgAc4mwdAmm3kZZ&index=11

Ocean documentary by David Attenborough – National Geographic - www.youtube.com/watch?v=v5J7aP2FYH4

Community gardens & sustainable food agencies

Community gardens

Community gardeners enjoy growing their own fruit and vegetables using sustainable organic horticultural practices and foster the sharing and development of a diverse set of gardening skills.

They are often very interested in growing fresh, local, organic food produce and very little ornamentals other than to attract bees. They also often have composting facilities as well as encourage sharing and swapping produce among the members and community.

North Fitzroy Community Gardens Group
https://rushallgarden.wordpress.com

Community food hubs

Community food hubs have a vision for:
- Sustainability - supporting a healthy environment, healthy people and a resilient community
- Just – making nutritious and culturally appropriate food accessible and affordable for everyone
- Vibrant – protecting and nurturing food culture, celebrates diversity and builds a sense of community

Community food hubs – like Community Food Hubs Merri-bek - https://conversations.merri-bek.vic.gov.au/community-food-hub-moreland

Other sustainable food agencies and markets

- Fresh foods at Australian Farmers Markets – https://farmersmarkets.org.au/
- Sustainable Table – *Action to enable resilient agricultural ecosystems, create thriving communities and reimagine economies* - www.sustainabletable.org.au/about
- Sustainability Victoria – *Shop sustainably for food* – www.sustainability.vic.gov.au/circular-economy-and-recycling/at-home/avoid-waste/shop-sustainably/food
- The Australian Food Network – *A network of citizen farmers, researchers, policy experts and community connectors on a mission to transform food* – https://sustain.org.au
- Australian Environmental Grant Makers Network – Sustainable food systems www.aegn.org.au/issue-and-solution/sustainable-food-systems/
- CSIRO – Australia's national science agency – *Reshaping Australian Food Systems* www.csiro.au/en/work-with-us/services/consultancy-strategic-advice-services/csiro-futures/agriculture-and-food/reshaping-australian-food-systems
- Food security in Australia video – National Library – www.youtube.com/watch?v=LH3ky9ADT60

Food security in Australia lecture – www.youtube.com/watch?v=baJetFSBfik

Families go hungry as food security worsens – www.youtube.com/watch?v=OGtJQkUIqBc

Greening the planet

Trees the forgotten heroes of our health. Human have destroyed vast amounts of forests, including millions of trees, other plants, fungi and wildlife. Our planet is suffering from this destruction, so it is up to us to try to regenerate the greening of our planet with millions more trees to help make the planet healthier. We need the trees for our own survival too, as they provide oxygen for us to breath.

Trees the forgotten heroes of our health – WWF
https://wwf.org.au/blogs/trees-the-forgotten-heroes-for-our-health/
CSIRO Greening our Cities – www.csiro.au/en/news/all/articles/2021/november/urban-greening
Clean Air and Urban Landscapes Hub - https://nespurban.edu.au/research-projects/urban-greening/

Landcare Australia

The *20 Million Trees Program* was part of the Australian Government's National Landcare Program. They planted 20 million native trees and understory across Australia, establishing healthy, self-sustaining tree-based ecosystems. One of the most important factors of any project within the program is improving habitat for native wildlife, including endangered or threatened species, and threatened ecological communities. The project had hands-on engagement with local communities and land-care groups, capture carbon, and contributed to a reduction in Australia's net greenhouse gas emissions.

Landcare Australia – https://landcareaustralia.org.au/project/20-million-trees-program/

Plant-a-tree Program

Plant-a-Tree is an ambitious regeneration project to restore the natural landscape and reconnecting habitats by linking small patches of remaining vegetation to create a 200km green corridor from inland to the coast. Plant-a-Tree grows critical habitat for native wildlife on historically cleared land in a Global Biodiversity Hotspot.

Carbon Neutral – https://carbonneutral.com.au/product/plant-a-tree-program-australia/

Greenfleet Australia

Greenfleet can help you take climate action by offsetting the carbon emissions you caused, by planting native biodiverse forests in Australia & New Zealand to remove those emissions on your behalf.

Greenfleet Australia -– www.greenfleet.com.au

Greening Australia

Greening Australia is an independent environmental enterprise. A national not-for-profit committed to restoring Australia's diverse landscapes and protecting biodiversity in ways that benefit communities, economies, and nature.

Green environments, planting trees of healthy oxygen to breath and encouraging gardens with trees and edible food and flowers to attract bees, can make for healthier communities, with trees and gardens, and backyards, and local playgrounds.

Urban environments with green roofs, walkways with trees, and green walls. Architecture that incorporates green living spaces. Some inner-city space planning with community spaces in high-rise, garden seats with BBQs and gardens for community engagement and sense of belonging.

Greening Australia – www.greeningaustralia.org.au/about-us/
Video - 25 Million Trees for Biodiversity – https://m.youtube.com/watch?v=2Dzp_epw9gc

Conscious consumerism

Conscious consumerism is the concept of every time we spend money, we are making a vote with our wallet, on the kind of world we want to support. It involves making informed intentional purchases, which align with one's values. You can simply ask yourself: *Do I really need this? How long will I use it for? Where was it made? Who made it? How far did it travel to be here and will it end up in landfill at the end of its life?*

Conscious consumerism can take many forms and be taken to many levels. You may choose to focus on a particular value, such as: being plastic-free, having a low carbon footprint or avoiding child labour. Or, you may want to include the whole package as the team at Clean + Conscious do, by choosing products which are ethical and sustainable in their materials, manufacturing and life cycle, as well as non-toxic in ingredients and materials, and made by brands who are socially responsible in giving back to their local and global communities.

Clean + Conscious – ethical & sustainable conscious consumerism
https://cleanandconscious.com.au/social-change/what-is-conscious-consumerism-and-why-does-it-matter/

Conscious consumerism – closer, fresher, better video – City of Morton Bay QLD –
www.youtube.com/watch?v=W7XK6FIXx9k

Ethical Clothing - Buy ethical, support local

Ethical Clothing Australia is an accreditation body, working collaboratively with local textile, clothing and footwear (TCF) businesses to protect and uphold the rights of Australian garment workers.

To be Ethical Clothing Australia accredited, a business's manufacturing operations are audited from design to dispatch to ensure that local TCF workers, including outworkers, are being paid appropriately, receiving all their legal entitlements and working in safe conditions.

By supporting an Ethical Clothing Australia accredited business you are helping to strengthen the Australian TCF industry and you're valuing the rights of our local garment workers

. Ethical Clothing Australia – https://ethicalclothingaustralia.org.au
Clothing the Gaps – Indigenous company – www.clothingthegaps.com.au
10 Ethical clothing brands – www.youtube.com/watch?v=5ql1wdOLgwc

Ethical Consumers Australia

Ethical Consumers Australia aims to work to make it easier for Australian consumers to make ethical consumption choices, and to overcome barriers faced by people who want to make ethical consumption choices. These choices could: favour a sustainable environment; protect or support human rights; increase social justice; or promote the interests and rights of animals.

Ethical Consumers Australia
https://consumersfederation.org.au/ethical-consumers-australia/#:~:text=Ethical%20Consumers%20Australia%20aims%20to,interests%20and%20rights%20of%20animals.

Ethical consumerism interview – Sky News – www.youtube.com/watch?v=US-q4C8ytbU

Renewable energy & recycling for a healthy planet

Energy Networks Australia
As Australia works toward net zero, Energy Networks Australia unites regulators, governments, and industry partners with our members to innovate and create cost-effective, sustainable energy solutions for all.

Connecting renewable energy to customers in an affordable and sustainable way. To decarbonise Australia's economy at least cost to customers, coal power must progressively exit the system and be replaced by firmed renewable generation. To continue to connect this new renewable generation at the pace required, we must prioritise partnerships, investment, and community understanding and support.

Energy Networks Australia – www.energynetworks.com.au
Australia's renewable energy sources video – www.youtube.com/watch?v=4WHp8wU18Xc

Australian Renewable Energy Agency
Australian Renewable Energy Agency supports the global transition to net zero emissions by accelerating the pace of pre-commercial innovation, to the benefit of Australian consumers, businesses and workers. They develop projects that can help accelerate renewable energy in Australia, spanning from early stage research in the lab, to demonstration projects in the field. They provide information and insights into the renewable energy industry.

Australian Renewable Energy Agency – https://arena.gov.au
Australian Renewable Energy Agency videos – www.youtube.com/c/AustralianRenewableEnergyAgency
Why Australia will be the world's new energy superpower – www.youtube.com/watch?v=kHA0pcMizQM
Australia pushing forward with renewable energy *green dream* – www.youtube.com/watch?v=wbya67xP-Cw

Benefits of electric bikes and cars
Globally, the transport sector produces about one quarter of greenhouse gas emissions. Finding cleaner ways to get around is necessary to combating the climate crisis. E-bikes also offer solutions to the problems of traffic congestion, fuel costs and sedentary lifestyles.

Electric bike right for you? – https://theconversation.com/is-an-electric-bike-right-for-you-heres-what-to-consider-before-you-buy-230024
Bicycle Network – https://bicyclenetwork.com.au/newsroom/2024/09/11/its-time-to-accept-e-bikes-for-what-they-are-electric-vehicles/
United Nations sustainable transport
www.un.org/sites/un2.un.org/files/media_gstc/FACT_SHEET_Climate_Change.pdf

Reduce, recycle & repair
Everything we buy and use in our daily lives has a carbon footprint: from its manufacture to its transport. Much of what we buy ends up in landfill, becomes litter, pollutes our oceans, contributes to the emission of greenhouse gases, or harms the planet in other ways. We need to cut our consumption to reduce our environmental impact. Single use items make no sense for our wallets or the environment.

52 Climate Actions – www.52climateactions.com/refuse-reduce-reuse-repair-recycle/full
The Circular Economy Hub – https://acehub.org.au/knowledge-hub/case-studies/fixable
Planet Ark – recycling near you – https://recyclingnearyou.com.au/reuse-hub/
Sustainability Victoria – repair hubs & cafes – www.sustainability.vic.gov.au/circular-economy/community-circular-economy-guides/guide-to-running-repair-hubs-and-cafes
Repair gardening tools Café, Sydney – Gardening Australia video – www.youtube.com/watch?v=-TRhnCPC8Xs

Living in harmony with nature

Transition Towns

Transition Towns are towns all over the globe, who are actively planning and striving to become sustainable and resilient, to be better prepared for the challenges ahead.

Transition Towns also called Earthwise Harmony in Australia, to promote back to nature with local community groups for community connectedness.

We can experience transcendent moments appreciating the wonders of nature, caring for the planet and caring for the local natural community. The Transition Network is movement of communities coming together to reimagine and rebuild our world.

Transition Network – https://transitionnetwork.org

Stories of change in Transition Towns – www.youtube.com/watch?v=izTtFiw0AiA

Global Ecovillage Network

The Global Ecovillage Network envisions a world of empowered citizens and communities, designing and implementing their own pathways to a sustainable future, and building bridges of hope and international solidarity.

Their mission to innovate, catalyse, educate and advocate in global partnership with ecovillages and all those dedicated to the shift to a regenerative world.

Global Ecovillage Network – https://ecovillage.org

Global Ecovillage Network video – www.youtube.com/watch?v=l1FSLEMmPZk

Eco-Villages Australia

Eco-villages are about connected and sustainable living, in a world where the land is often suffering and people can be disconnected.

Eco Villages Australia (EVA) is a non-profit organisation that provides the legal and financial model to create collaborative housing eco-communities, often for small groups of people, say 5 -15, to restore and care for the land that they inhabit.

In these communities, residents become stewards and caretakers of the land as they work co-operatively, make decisions, and take responsibility for their ecological sustainability, social prosperity and economic viability. EVA has been carbon neutral from inception. The first eco-village site was purchased in 2019 in Maleny, Queensland.

This is a unique model, called: *Collective Stewardship*.

Eco-Villages Australia – www.ecovillages.au

Inside Australia's hidden ecovillage video – www.youtube.com/watch?v=TGpvuza2rkE

Ecovillage Pioneers Australia – Permaculture video – www.youtube.com/watch?v=1m5rSTVlV-A

Inside The Paddock ecovillage, Castlemaine, Vic – www.youtube.com/watch?v=bbhm9Eho9iA

Saving our natural habitats

Trust for Nature

Trust for Nature has been protecting ecosystems and wildlife on private land in Victoria for over 50 years,

From the state's majestic forests to its enchanting deserts, from its breathtaking coasts to its highest peaks, we work in partnership with local communities, Traditional Owners, scientists and landowners to preserve and enhance the habitats of threatened and endangered species of plants and animals.

In Victoria, 62% of the land is privately owned, so working with private landholders is critical to secure the future of our unique ecosystems and species. To date, more than 110,000 hectares of private land has been protected in the state of Victoria.

Across their 40+ nature reserves, and 1500+ properties owned by individuals, The Trust for Nature team helps restore, preserve and improve habitats, engaging with local communities and Traditional Owners to share knowledge, restore cultural practices and generate greater outcomes for Victoria's unique plant and animal species. The work is guided by a Statewide Conservation Plan, which provides a scientific framework to inform the conservation strategy.

Trust for Nature – https://trustfornature.org.au

Trust for Nature – Conservation properties for sale
https://trustfornature.org.au/properties/?jsf=bricks-query-loop&tax=property-category:revolving-fund

Private landholders protecting Victoria's natural wonder – Trust for Nature Victoria – www.youtube.com/watch?v=Wn1moOnmh30

Deep nature connection: Caring for nature in crisis lecture – Trust for Nature Victoria – www.youtube.com/watch?app=desktop&v=zdIlmDpqrnU

Save the Great Barrier Reef

The Great Barrier Reef is the largest living structure on the planet, with over 2,900 individual reefs and 900 islands, stretching over 2,300k long, located in the Coral Sea off the Queensland coast. It can be seen from outer-space. In 1998, a mass coral bleaching event devastated the Great Barrier Reef, killing one in 12 of the world's corals. In response, the Great Barrier Reef Foundation was created to find and grow the best solutions to protect the world's greatest reef.

Great Barrier Reef Foundation – www.barrierreef.org

Australian Government Protecting the Great Barrier Reef – www.dcceew.gov.au/parks-heritage/great-barrier-reef/protecting

How scientists are restoring the Great Barrier Reef – www.youtube.com/watch?v=8hknaJQRh8s

Clean up Australia

Clean up Australia inspires and mobilises communities to improve and conserve our environment, eliminate litter and end waste. Clean Up Australia has evolved to provide practical solutions to help all Australians live more sustainably every day of the year.

Join a Clean Up Australia event – https://register.cleanup.org.au/join-a-clean-up

Clean up Australia 2021 – Behind the News – www.youtube.com/watch?v=W8B3ErkVT1k

CHALLENGERS for personal climate change actions

CHALLENGE FOR CLIMATE 2025
CLIMATE ACTION IDEAS

CLIMATE ACTION ISN'T A RIGID CHECKLIST. WE DEFINE IT BROADLY: ANYTHING THAT SPREADS AWARENESS, SHOWS COMPASSION FOR OUR PLANET, OR MOVES US TOWARDS A MORE SUSTAINABLE FUTURE. YOUR ACTION COULD BE A CONVERSATION, A PERSONAL CHANGE, A MOMENT OF LEARNING, OR WHATEVER FEELS MEANINGFUL TO YOU. LET YOUR CREATIVITY LEAD THE WAY.

(5 minute action) (20 minute action) (1 hour + action)

Community	Citizen	Individual
Share a social media post	Sign a petition	Have a fully plant-based day
Ask a friend or family member to host a Climate Conversation	Research your vote and consider who the most climate-friendly candidate in your electorate is	Switch your fuel vehicle commute to public transport, walking, or cycling
Order a climate related sign for your window or front yard	Write an email to your local MP using an MPEGs template	Write to a business that you have/plan to boycott, explaining your reasons for not purchasing their products
Have a climate chat with a friend, family member, or colleague	Call your local MP's office using an MPEGs template	Research and switch your bank or superannuation account
Talk to your manager about having Climate for Change deliver a workplace training for your organisation	Write an email to the Minister for Climate Change or Minister for Environment	Research and initiate switching to green energy in your home
Schedule and plan to host a Climate Conversation	Write an email to one of your state or territory's senators using an MPEGs template	Rewild your backyard or balcony by planting local, native plants that are good for pollinators, and contribute to reducing urban heat
Work on the online Climate Conversations facilitator course	Take part in a rally or protest	Install a water saving device in your shower

Challenge for Climate– Climate Conversations Program – https://challengeforclimate.com

CHALLENGERS for workplace climate change actions

CHALLENGE FOR CLIMATE 2025
WORKPLACE GUIDE

EVERY WORKPLACE IS DIFFERENT – USE THESE IDEAS TO SPARK CLIMATE ACTION IN A WAY THAT FITS YOUR CULTURE!

QUESTIONS TO CONSIDER:
- What sustainability initiatives already exist?
- Who might be interested in joining you?
- What resources/support could your workplace offer?
- How can you make it engaging for your colleagues?

MAKING IT COMPETITIVE

Teams raise 4x more on average! Some team ideas to boost engagement:
- Department vs Department leaderboard
- Front of house vs back of house
- Opening vs closing shifts compete
- Inter-venue challenges
- New Starters vs Veterans
- Management vs Staff

TEMPLATE

> Hey team! 👋 I'm taking part in this cool challenge in April - 10 climate actions in 10 days, https://challengeforclimate.com/ - and thought it could be fun to do together! Think team competitions, themed days, maybe some friendly forfeits for losing teams (kitchen duties?). Could be a great way to make a difference while having some fun together. Let me know if you're interested and we can grab a coffee to chat more!

THEME DAY IDEAS:
- Transport Tuesday (sustainable commuting)
- **Waste-Free Wednesday** (zero waste lunch)
- Finance Friday (super/banking switches)
- **Meat-Free Monday** (plant-based meals)
- Keep Cup Challenge (week-long commitment)
- **Leftover Legends Day**
- Local Supplier Tuesday (highlight producers)
- Food Waste Friday (composting focus)
- Switch-Off Sunday (digital detox)
- Power-Down Friday (energy focus)
- **Talk-About-It Tuesday** (climate conversations)

HOW TO ENGAGE

Consider somewhere to track actions daily physically or virtually, and if doing teams incentives go a long way (who's on dishwasher duty?!)

1. **Team Meetings**
   - Share your challenge journey
   - Ask for a 5-minute slot in regular meetings
2. **Internal Communications**
   - Post updates on Slack/Teams
   - Share in company newsletter
   - Update/share challenge email signature
   - Add to intranet announcements
3. **Visual Presence**
   - Set up a challenge board in common areas
   - Share daily climate facts/tips
   - Celebrate team achievements

WANT MORE SUPPORT?

Check out our website the workplace conversations & workshops we can provide

 @climateforchangeau
climateforchange.org.au

#CHALLENGEFORCLIMATE

Climate for Change – www.climateforchange.org.au

> **Reasons to love our earth**
> Our planet is in the perfect position to support life on earth
> Earth can teach us a thing or two about recycling
> The oceans and trees provide us with oxygen
> We can take deep, cleansing breaths
> Earth provides a solid ground to stand on
> Our planet holds such mystery and enchantment
>
> 8 Reasons to love our earth – Greenhous Culture
> https://greenhouseculture.ie/the-takeover/8-good-reasons-to-love-our-earth/

Planner for Climate Change actions

Community	Citizen	Individual	Workplace
eg. social media share, climate conversation in person, group, or online.	eg. Sign a petition, vote for carer of environment, contact local MP, join a peaceful protest	eg. Plant-based day, boycott a business, change to green energy, water saving device	eg. sustainability initiative, waste free, meat free days.

Consider walking and using public transport more, such as taking the bus or train in the morning, hoping to contribute to a world where some personal inconvenience is normalised for the sake of protecting the planet. Hoping to help lead to needing less space for roads and carparks, with more funding for natural rewilding, where creatures and people are less at risk of being killed by cars, and a culture where people get to know familiar faces in their community and chat more with neighbours.

Visiting Victor Harbour, SA in 2024, where first child was born in late 70s.

Climate Change Solutions video – Australian Museum – www.youtube.com/watch?v=9FjcePzrKa0

Regenerative practices and climate justice – https://www.youtube.com/watch?v=Gk15fWAA3F0

Climate integrity summit 2024 - www.youtube.com/watch?v=y8K6Ojty1iw

May we give our planet much tender loving care,
so our planet can continue
to give our children and generations to come,
much tender loving care in return.

References

Attenborough, D. (2021). *A life on our planet: My witness statement and a vision for the future*. Penguin Books

Baird, J. (2020). *Phosphorescence: On awe, wonder and things that sustain you when the world goes dark.* Harper-Collins Australia.

Baird, J. (2023). *Bright shining: How grace changes everything.* Fourth Estate Australia.

Bevis, M., Atkinson, J., McCarthy, L., & Sweet, M. (2020). Kungas' trauma experiences and effects on behaviour in Central Australia. (Research report, 03/2020). ANROWS.

Blackie, S. (2018). *The enchanted life: Unlocking the magic of the everyday.* House of Anansi Press.

Burke, S. (2017). *The climate change empowerment handbook: Psychological strategies to tackle climate change.* Australian Psychological Society.

Burke, S. (2020). The space between hope and despair. *Dumb Feather*, 13 Jan, 2020. https://www.dumbofeather.com/articles/the-space-between-hope-and-despair/

Devlin, J. (1999). *Leonard Cohen: In his own words.* Omnibus Press

Deverell, G. W., & Pattel-Gray, A. (2023). *Contemplating country: More Gondwana theology.* Wipf & Stock.

De Waal, F. (2006). *Primates and philosophers: How morality evolved.* Princeton University Press.

Edwards, T., & Chiera, C. (2019). *The freedom of virtue: Navigating excellence in the art of living amongst a world of instant gratification.* Australian Academic Press.

Fuller, A. (2025). Neuroadvantage: *The strength-based approach to neurodivergence.* Amba Press

Goldstein, A.M. (2009). The charms of nature: Darwin on meaning and value. *Evolution: Education and Outreach, 2, 326–333.*

Hepper, E. G., Wildschut, T., Sedikides, C., Robertson, S., & Routledge, C. D. (2020). *Time capsule: Nostalgia shields psychological wellbeing from limited time horizons. Emotion.* American Psychological Association.

Karapanagiotidis, K. (2018). *The power of hope. Riverhead Books.* Harpers Collins Publishers.

Keltner, D. & Haidt, J. (2003). Approaching awe, a moral, spiritual, and aesthetic emotion. *Cognition and Emotion*, 17:2, 297-314.

Keltner, D. (2023). *Awe: The transformative power of everyday wonder.* Allen Lane, Penguin Books.

Levine, G. (2008). *Darwin loves you: Natural selection and the re-enchantment of the world.* Princeton University Press.

Mackay, H. (2021). *The kindness revolution: How we can restore hope, rebuild trust and inspire optimism.* Allen & Unwin.

McInerney, J. (2010). Review of "Creation," a film by Jon Amiel. *Genetics in Medicine* 12, 182–183.

Morsillo, J & Fisher, A. (2007). Appreciative inquiry with youth to create meaningful community projects. The Australian Community Psychologist, 19, pp.47;61.

Morsillo, J & Fisher, A. (2009). "Appreciative inquiry with migrant youth for meaningful community projects." Book chapter in M. F. Hindsworth & T. B. Lang (Eds). *Community Participation and Empowerment*. Nova Publishers.

Morsillo, J. (2016) Seeking Sanctuary paper in *Academic* (unpublished). - www.academia.edu/38189126/Seeking_Sanctuary

Morsillo, J. (2024). *Sing me a song to soar: Finding hope in our redemptive stories.* Wipf & Stock Resource Pub.

Rose, M. (2002). *Dadirri: Inner deep listening and quiet stillness.* Emmaus Productions.

Routledge C., Arndt, J., Wildschut, T., Sedikides, C., Hart, C., Juhl, J., Vingerhoets, A. J., & Scholtz, W. (2011). The past makes the present meaningful: Nostalgia as an existential resource. *Journal of Personality and Social Psychology*, 101, 638-652.

Routledge, C., Wildschut, T., Sedikides, C., & Juhl, J. (2013). Nostalgia as a resource for psychological health and well-being. *Social and Personality Psychology Compass*, 7, 808-818.

Schumarcher, E.F. (1973) *Small is beautiful: A study of economics as if people matter*. Vintage Books.

Schwartz, S. H. (2012). An Overview of the Schwartz Theory of Basic Values. *Online Readings in Psychology and Culture*, 2(1).

Singer, P. (2009). *The life you can save: How to do your part to end world poverty*. The life you can save.

Thunberg, G. (2019). *No one is too small to make a difference.* Random House.

United Nations (2025) *United Nations: Peace, Dignity and Unity on a healthy planet.* United Nations Declaration of Human Rights. Website: www.un.org/en/about-us/universal-declaration-of-human-rights

Helpful websites on human rights

Action Network – Love makes a way – Christians advocating for asylum seekers – https://actionnetwork.org/groups/love-makes-a-way-australia
Anti-slavery Australia – https://antislavery.org.au
Ask Izzy – https://askizzy.org.au
Asylum Seeker Resource Centre – Melbourne - https://asrc.org.au
Australian Greens Party – greening planet & abolish offshore detention – https://greens.org.au
Australian Human Rights Commission – https://humanrights.gov.au/our-work/
Australian Museum – Genocide – https://australian.museum/learn/first-nations/genocide-in-australia/
Big hART, Tasmania – www.bighart.org
Birthing Kit Foundation – www.bkfa.org.au
Black lives matter – https://blacklivesmatter.com
Brotherhood of St Lawrence – www.bsl.org.au
Centre for information on justice and peace – https://centerfjp.org/article-posts/formation-and-justice-in-micah-68/
Common Grace – on Jesus & Justice – www.commongrace.org.au
Community choir – Community Music Vic – https://cmvic.org.au/groups
Community Gardens Australia – https://communitygarden.org.au
Creative Spirits – www.creativespirits.info/aboriginalculture/law/juvenile-detention
Curly Tales – Five positive things amidst the Covid-19 outbreak https://curlytales.com/5-positive-things-amidst-covid-19-outbreak-that-prove-that-the-earth- is-healing/
Deadly Story – Indigenous history – https://deadlystory.com/page/culture/history/Frontier_wars
Dolly Parton's Imagination Library – https://imaginationlibrary.com/au/
Faith Communities Council of Victoria – www.faithvictoria.org.au
Fearless Women ,ACT – https://fearlesswomen.org.au
Food Bank – ending hunger in Australia – www.foodbank.org.au/?state=vic
Genocide in Australia – https://australian.museum/learn/first-nations/genocide-in-australia/
Good Shepherd – Youth Homelessness – https://goodshep.org.au/services/youth-homelessness-service-vic/
Graham Kendrick. Copyright © 1993 Make Way Music – www.grahamkendrick.co.uk
Human Rights Watch – www.hrw.org/news/2016/06/21/australia-where-parties-stand-human-rights
Katherine Isolated Children's Services in partnership with Dolly' Imagination Library https://imaginationlibrary.com/au/affiliate/katherinent/
Kindness Pandemic – www.thekindnesspandemic.org
Koorie Curriculum – early childhood education for Australian Indigenous children https://kooricurriculum.com
Kumon Global (Australia) tutoring - https://au.kumonglobal.com
McKillop Family Services – www.mackillop.org.au
Metoo Movement – https://metoomvmt.org/get-to-know-us/history-inception/
Mission Australia – www.missionaustralia.com.au/about-us
National Disability Insurance Service (NDIS) – www.ndis.gov.au
Open Food Network – https://openfoodnetwork.org.au/
Oxfam report - www.oxfam.org.au/2025/01/takers-not-makers-how-billionaires-profit-while-billions-struggle/amp/)
Prison Network – www.prisonnetwork.org.au
Refugee Council of Australia – www.refugeecouncil.org.au/education-info/3/
Smith Family – www.thesmithfamily.com.au
SNAICC – National Voice for Australian Indigenous children – www.snaicc.org.au
Stars Foundation – Mentoring Indigenous girls - https://starsfoundation.org.au
Tear Fund – End poverty –www.tearfund.org.au/stories/good-news-that-restores
The life you can save Australia – How to do your part to end poverty – www.thelifeyoucansave.org.au
TEFL –– Teach English as second language – Australia or overseas or online courses www.tefl.org/en-us/about-us/
Ubuntu – www.afnconference.org.au/ubuntu-i-am-because-you-are/
UNESCO – www.unesco.org/en/articles/afghanistan-14-million-girls-still-banned-school-de-facto-authorities
United Nations Declaration of Human Rights – www.un.org/en/about-us/universal-declaration-of-human-rights.#

Caring for the planet

Australia Conservation Foundation (ACF) – www.acf.org.au
Australian Environmental Grant Makers Network –
    www.aegn.org.au/issue-and-solution/sustainable-food-systems/
Australian Food Network – https://sustain.org.au
Australian Greens Party – https://greens.org.au
Australian Youth Climate Coalition – www.aycc.org.au
Bicycle Network - https://bicyclenetwork.com.au/newsroom/2024/09/11/its-time-to-accept-e-bikes-for-what-they-are-electric-vehicles/
Bushcare and Landcare volunteering – www.aabr.org.au/volunteering/bushcare-and-landcare-volunteering/
Bob Brown Foundation – https://bobbrown.org.au
Bicycle Network – https://bicyclenetwork.com.au/newsroom/2024/09/11/its-time-to-accept-e-bikes-for-what-they-are-electric-vehicles/
Callaghan, P., & Gordon, P. (2022). *The dreaming path: Indigenous thinking to change your life.* Pantera Press
Clean Air and Urban Landscapes Hub – https://nespurban.edu.au/research-projects/urban-greening/
Clean + Conscious – https://cleanandconscious.com.au/social-change/what-is-conscious-consumerism-and-why-does-it-matter/
Climate change article – www.dumbofeather.com/articles/the-space-between-hope-and-despair/
Climate for Change – Challenge for Climate – www.climateforchange.org.au
Clothing the gaps – Indigenous company – www.clothingthegaps.com.au
Community Gardens Australia – https://communitygarden.org.au
Creation: The story of Charles Darwin movie 2009 – www.dailymotion.com/video/x96rkys
CSIRO Greening our Cities – www.csiro.au/en/news/all/articles/2021/november/urban-greening
David Attenborough & Greta Thunberg interview – https://youtu.be/-pP7M20iNsc
Eco-villages Australia – www.ecovillages.au
Environmental psychology – Dr Suzie Burke - Australian Psychological Society -
    https://psychology.org.au/getmedia/88ee1716-2604-44ce-b87a-ca0408dfaa12/climate-change-empowerment-handbook.pdf & www.dumbofeather.com/articles/the-space-between-hope-and-despair/
Fresh foods at Australian Farmers Markets – https://farmersmarkets.org.au/
Friends of the Earth Australia – www.foe.org.au/who_we_are
Global Ecovillage Network – https://ecovillage.org
Greenpeace Australia Pacific – www.greenpeace.org.au/about-us/
Greta Thunberg activist – BBC - www.bbc.com/news/world-europe-49918719
Indigenous healing programs - https://healingfoundation.org.au/app/uploads/2017/02/Aboriginal-and-Torres-Strait-Islander-Healing-Programs-A-Literature-Review.pdf
Jane Goodall Institute – https://janegoodall.org
Nature Based Therapy – www.naturebasedtherapy.com.au
North Fitzroy Community Gardens Group – https://rushallgarden.wordpress.com
Transition Network – https://transitionnetwork
Sharing two world views of nature's healing – www.metaphoricallyspeaking.com.au/two-world-views/
Sustainable Table – www.sustainabletable.org.au/about
Sustainability Victoria – www.sustainability.vic.gov.au/circular-economy-and-recycling/at-home/avoid-waste/shop-sustainably/food
Transition Towns – Stories of change – https://transitionnetwork.org/news/collecting-stories-of-community-led-change/
Trust for Nature – https://trustfornature.org.au
United Nations sustainable transport -
    www.un.org/sites/un2.un.org/files/media_gstc/FACT_SHEET_Climate_Change.pdf
World Wildlife Fund (WWF) Australia – wwf.org.au/about-us
World Wildlife Fund – Sir David Attenborough – www.worldwildlife.org/videos/sir-david-attenborough-explains-why-we-need-a-new-global-deal-to-protect-our-ocean.#

Background & impact of ultra-rich ruling the world

Australia's 50 Richest 2025: Tech billionaires propel wealth surge as mining fortunes slip – Forbes magazine – www.forbes.com/sites/naazneenkarmali/2025/02/12/australias-50-richest-2025-tech-billionaires-propel-wealth-surge-as-mining-fortunes-slip/

Australia's richest woman – www.theguardian.com/australia-news/2025/mar/31/a-female-donald-trump-how-gina-rinehart-is-pushing-trumps-message-australia-ntwnfb

Billionaires rule – Foreign Policy - https://foreignpolicy.com/2025/03/25/billionaire-rule-foreign-policy-magazine-print-2025-issue/

Billionaires wealth worldwide – Oxfam International – www.oxfam.org/en/press-releases/billionaire-wealth-surges-2-trillion-2024-three-times-faster-year-while-number

Business' empire is built on 38 billion in government funding. The Washington Post – 26 Feb, 2025 – www.washingtonpost.com/technology/interactive/2025/elon-musk-business-government-contracts-funding/

Dismantling of democracy in USA by Prof Arjun Appadurai
www.theguardian.com/us-news/ng-interactive/2025/may/25/trump-american-democracy

European Training Foundation – Impact of USAID withdrawal – www.etf.europa.eu/sites/default/files/2025-04/USAID%20doc%20%282%29.pdf

Impact of savagery. What they are doing is cruel and lethal – Tim Costello – https://publicchristianity.org/article/ive-seen-the-impact-of-trump-and-musks-savagery-what-theyre-doing-is-cruel-and-lethal/ [More articles by Tim Costello - https://publicchristianity.org/author/timcostello/]

Is this the beginning of the end of the American empire? – Sydney Morning Herald video – www.youtube.com/watch?v=vWHkTLzeGPk

Mass government cuts could make private companies millions. The Guardian, 16 Feb 2025 – www.theguardian.com/technology/2025/feb/16/elon-musk-doge-government-privatization?CMP=Share_iOSApp_Other

Oligarchy countries in the world and their impact – World Population Review – https://worldpopulationreview.com/country-rankings/oligarchy-countries#the-impact-of-an-oligarchy-government-on-its-people

Oxfam community agency report, Jan 2025 – www.oxfam.org.au/2025/01/takers-not-makers-how-billionaires-profit-while-billions-struggle/amp/

Richest men take on poorest children, New York Times, 5 Feb 2025 – www.nytimes.com/2025/02/05/opinion/usaid-spending-trump-musk.html

Rich men rule the world – Wired – www.wired.com/story/editor-letter-rich-men-rule-the-world/

Slashing federal spending – by Soo Rin Kim, ABC News , 10 Feb, 2025 - https://abcnews.go.com/amp/US/musk-works-slash-federal-spending-firms-received-billions/story?id=118589121

Takers not makers: How billionaires profit – Oxfam report, 2025 – https://www.oxfam.org.au/2025/01/takers-not-makers-how-billionaires-profit-while-billions-struggle/amp/

The secession of the billionaire class – Prof Robert Reich, 22 April, 2025 – https://robertreich.substack.com/p/the-secession-of-the-billionaire

To spurn empathy is to spur evil – by Dr Julia Baird – The Sydney Morning Herald, 7 March 2025. – www.smh.com.au/lifestyle/life-and-relationships/elon-musk-is-wrong-to-spurn-empathy-is-to-spur-evil-20250307-p5lhpr.html

Trump is dismantling democracy – US Senate video – www.youtube.com/watch?v=7aDbEmHo9Fo

Unjust poverty and unearned wealth – Oxfam report
– www.oxfam.org/en/takers-not-makers-unjust-poverty-and-unearned-wealth-colonialism

USAID withdrawal: In three month's half of them will be dead – Hana Kiros, The Atlantic, 16 April, 2025 – www.theatlantic.com/health/archive/2025/04/usaid-doge-children-starvation/682484/

Songs for life

All are welcome in this place – Let us build a place where love can dwell – Martin Haugen–
www.youtube.com/watch?v=FhPnjA7wsIY*

All things bright and beautiful all creatures great and small – Cecil Frances Alexander –
www.youtube.com/watch?v=FT_oDqOEGpc and
RSPCA Animal walk advertisement – www.youtube.com/watch?v=vO5qXw-WTDk * **

Amazing grace – John Newton - history – www.cbsnews.com/news/the-story-of-amazing-grace/ *

Beauty for brokenness – God of the poor – Graham Kendrick – www.youtube.com/watch?v=pPvioAt5fq4c *

Blackbird singing in the dead of night – Paul McCartney
– https://americansongwriter.com/meaning-blackbird-the-beatles-song-lyrics/

Bridge over troubled waters – Paul Simon – www.youtube.com/watch?v=h0n-mYqB9WQ *

Brother, sister let me serve you – Richard Gillard – www.youtube.com/watch?v=0JahFRDrSCs *

Finding a home – We are pilgrims, we are strangers – Ross Langmead –
www.rosslangmead.com/Downloads/SongsMP3/WeArePilgrims.mp3 *

Grace Road – Philip Hudson for Sorry Day 2016 – www.youtube.com/watch?v=-Mo_OUsbIMc

Gracias a la vida – *Thank you for life* – Violeta Parra – www.youtube.com/watch?v=jAlKfFLFnRI

Grateful: A love song to the world – Nimo Patel & Daniel Nahmod – www.youtube.com/watch?v=sO2o98Zpzg8

Heal the world – Michael Jackson – www.youtube.com/watch?v=GBATSkfpOTc

I believe in the people of all nations – Andrea Botcelli – www.youtube.com/watch?v=ABj7gxsbAjY

Imagine all the people living life as one – John Lennon – www.youtube.com/watch?v=bNnFFKv_NyI

Lift up your voice and sing – Black Anthem for civil rights movement – J. Rosamond Johnson and James Weldon
Johnson – www.youtube.com/watch?v=gGsZqCTrQAs

Light a candle for peace – Shelley Murley - www.youtube.com/watch?v=8B8vuFngtrU

Light a candle instead of cursing the darkness – Suzette Hertz

Lean on me when you're not strong – Bill Withers – www.youtube.com/watch?v=Nx_D0VTHBag

Lord let me see, see the beauty of the person, not the colour of their skin – Prof Ross Langmead –
www.youtube.com/watch?v=8z8roH9ocFM *

Make me a channel of your peace – *maybe* Fr. Esther Bouquerel – www.youtube.com/watch?v=fYz14jEoaeU*

May my life be a prayer – Julie Morsillo – Brunswick Baptist Church Songbook *

My city of ruins – Come on rise up – Bruce Springsteen – www.youtube.com/watch?v=

One world – I'm going to take care of the world – Becky Drake & Sleadford Girls Brigade –
www.youtube.com/watch?v=SEOltHwQrDw **

One world, one song – World Hunger Day UK 2013 – Sullivan Duntra – www.youtube.com/watch?v=fboiyuZP7Sg

Peace for a world that is crying – Julie Morsillo – Brunswick Baptist Church Songbook

Take care of the world – Karen Daniel – www.youtube.com/watch?v=4lFtADNdsqA

That's what friends are for – In good time and bad times I'll be on your side forever more – Carole Bayer Sager &
Burt Bacharach – www.youtube.com/watch?v=Ljpg16lE5mw

The prayer – David Foster, Carole Bayer Sager, Tony Reni & Alberto Testa – www.youtube.com/watch?v=IDsyvKJZz7g *

Took the children away – Archie Roach – www.youtube.com/watch?v=IL_DBNkkcSE

We are Australian – Bruce Woodley & Dobe Newton – www.youtube.com/watch?v=Hd473yG-jiw

We are the world, we are the children – Michael Jackson & Lionel Richie – www.britannica.com/topic/We-Are-
the-World **and** www.youtube.com/watch?v=9AjkUyX0rVw

We shall overcome some day – traditional – www.kennedy-center.org/education/resources-for-educators/classroom-
resources/media-and-interactives/media/music/story-behind-the-song/the-story-behind-the-song/we-shall-overcome/

What a wonderful world – Bob Thiele (as George Douglas) & George David Weiss -
www.smoothradio.com/features/louis-armstrong-what-a-wonderful-world-facts/ **

You don't speak for me – Judy Small AM – www.youtube.com/watch?v=DEzt1B2Oo9A

You'll never walk alone – Richard Rodgers & Oscar Hammerstein – www.youtube.com/watch?v=kOHua5B_nqc

You're the voice – Keith Reid & co– sung by John Farnham – www.youtube.com/watch?v=fa3YDYhUYM0

*Songs with **Christian or spiritual** overtones.   ** Songs specifically for caring of **nature**

> Speak up for those who cannot speak for themselves,
> protect the rights of those who are helpless.
> Speak out and pronounce a sentence of justice,
> defend the cause of the wretched and the poor.
> *(Proverbs 31:8-9)*

Julie in garden studio

Acknowledgements

Thanks to Matt Wimer, Managing Editor of Wipf & Stock, for his trust in me, to complete another handbook. Enticing artwork of front cover again, by Shannon Carter, Wipf & Stock.

Thanks to colleagues who gave me feedback and editing advice for improvements, especially: Chara Meridith, plus Elise Bryant, Colleen Turner, Dr Lyn O'Grady, Janelle Brooks, Jeanine Batty, Julie Freeman, Catriona Milne, and Dr David Morsillo.

Thanks to all those, who over the years, have taught me about the need to advocate for the human rights of those who are most oppressed, especially: Prof Mark Brett and the late Prof Ross Langmead at Whitley College; Rev Tim Costello AO at Collins St Baptist; Moira Rayner at the Victorian Equal Opportunity Commission; Lyn Harasymiw at Victorian Public Service; Dr David Denborough and Cheryl White at Dulwich Centre, Adelaide; Kon Karapanagiotidis OAM and Dr Joan Beckwith at the Asylum Seeker Resource Centre; Prof Ron Adams, Prof Isaac Prilleltensky and Heather Gridley OAM at Victoria University and at the Australian Psychological Society (APS); Australian Indigenous Psychologists at APS; Liz Morrigan, psychologist and narrative therapist; Steve Bradbury at Eastern College Australia (formally Tabor) and former Director of Tear Fund; Rev Dr Garry Deverall, Indigenous theologian; Philip Hudson, songwriter on human rights at Brunswick Baptist Church.

Thanks for all the encouragement from my colleagues, graduate students, friends and family, including my two adult sons, grand-daughter, and husband of 50 years, Robert Morsillo.

Thanks everyone, *Dr Julie Morsillo – drjulie.morsillo@gmail.com*

Copyright Permissions

Quotes with referencing all used with permission from: *The Advocate for Human Rights (2025)* website image, www.theadvocatesforhumanrights.org/. *Dadirri (Deep Listening)* from Miriam Rose Foundation copyright@2025, www.miriamrosefoundation.org.au and photo. *Kungas' trauma experiences* (2020) article by Miriam Bevis. *Phosphorescence (2020)* and *Bright Shining (2023)* books by Dr Julia Baird. *The power of hope* (2018) by Kon Karapanagiotidis. *The Kindness Revolution* (2021) book by Prof Hugh Mackay. *Neuroadvantage* (2025) book by Dr Andrew Fuller. *Fearless Women (2025)* website and photo, https://fearlesswomen.org.au. *Stars Foundation* (2025) website, https://starsfoundation.org.au, permission given by Dr David Morawetz. *Prison Network* (2025) website, www.prisonnetwork.org.au and logo. *Alliance for Gambling Reform (2025)*, www.agr.org.au/ and *Gambling and social cohesion* article (2024) by Rev Dr Tim Costello AO. *Schwartz Theory of Basic Values* (2012) by Prof Shalom Schwartz. Big *h*ART Tasmania (2025) website, www.bighart.org. *Awe* (2023) book by Prof Dacher Kelter. *Climate Change Empowerment Handbook* (2023) and article on *The space between hope and despair (2020)* by Dr Susie Burke. *Climate for Change* tables on website, www.climateforchange.org.au. Every effort has been made to trace copyright holders in all the copyrighted materials in this handbook. The Publisher regrets any oversight and will be pleased to rectify any omission in future editions.

www.ingramcontent.com/pod-product-compliance
Lightning Source LLC
Chambersburg PA
CBHW080455170426
43196CB00016B/2811